At Issue

| Minorities and the Law

Other Books in the At Issue Series:

Animal Experimentation

Are Abortion Rights Threatened?

Are Teen Boot Camps Effective?

Are Unions Still Relevant?

Child Pornography

The Children of Undocumented Immigrants

Club Drugs

Digitized Textbooks

Divorce and Children

Fast Food

Fracking

High School Dropouts

How Far Should Science Extend the Human Lifespan?

Is China's Economic Growth a Threat to America?

Organic Food

Reality TV

The Right to Die

Sexting

Super PACs

Transgender People

Vaccines

What Are the Jobs of the Future?

At Issue

Minorities and the Law

Noël Merino, Book Editor

GREENHAVEN PRESS
A part of Gale, Cengage Learning

GALE
CENGAGE Learning·

Farmington Hills, Mich • San Francisco • New York • Waterville, Maine
Meriden, Conn • Mason, Ohio • Chicago

GALE
CENGAGE Learning

Patricia Coryell, *Vice President & Publisher, New Products & GVRL*
Douglas Dentino, *Manager, New Products*
Judy Galens, *Acquisitions Editor*

For more information, contact:
Greenhaven Press
27500 Drake Rd.
Farmington Hills, MI 48331-3535
Or you can visit our Internet site at gale.cengage.com

Articles in Greenhaven Press anthologies are often edited for length to meet page requirements. In addition, original titles of these works are changed to clearly present the main thesis and to explicitly indicate the author's opinion. Every effort is made to ensure that Greenhaven Press accurately reflects the original intent of the authors. Every effort has been made to trace the owners of copyrighted material.

LIBRARY OF CONGRESS CATALOGING-IN-PUBLICATION DATA

Minorities and the law / Noël Merino, book editor.
    pages cm. -- (At issue)
    Includes bibliographical references and index.
    ISBN 978-0-7377-7179-4 (hardcover) -- ISBN 978-0-7377-7180-0 (pbk.)
    1. Minorities--United States--Social conditions. 2. Justice, Administration of--United States. 3. Human rights--United States. I. Merino, Noël.
    E184.A1M5435 2015
    323.11--dc23
                                                           2014030225

Printed in Mexico
2 3 4 5 6 7 19 18 17 16 15

Contents

Introduction   7

1. Prison's Dilemma   10
   Glenn C. Loury

2. The Criminal Justice System Is Not   16
   Unfair to Minorities
   John Perazzo

3. The War on Marijuana in Black   21
   and White
   American Civil Liberties Union

4. The Policy of Stop-and-Frisk Targets   29
   Young Men of Color
   Scott Stringer

5. Stop-and-Frisk Protects Minorities   36
   Michael Barone

6. Minimum-Wage Madness   40
   Thomas Sowell

7. A Higher Minimum Wage Will Not Hurt   44
   Minorities or Eliminate Jobs
   Richard Eskow

8. Opposition to Voter ID Laws Is Insulting   49
   to Minorities
   David Limbaugh

9. Voter ID Laws Disenfranchise   53
   Minority Voters
   Jeremiah Goulka

10. The US Supreme Court Erred in Revising   62
    the Voting Rights Act
    Andrew Cohen

11. The US Supreme Court Was Correct to   70
    Revise the Voting Rights Act
    Hans A. von Spakovsky

12. Where Do Americans Stand   81
    on Affirmative Action?
    Jamelle Bouie

13. Do Race Preferences Help Students?   85
    Richard Sander and Stuart Taylor Jr.

14. The Next Affirmative Action   90
    Kevin Carey

15. Affirmative Action Should Be Based   97
    on Hardship Not Race
    Ben Carson

Organizations to Contact   101

Bibliography   105

Index   111

Introduction

Members of minority groups have not always fared well under the law. Slavery in the United States is a prime example of how a minority group was both created and kept powerless: African Americans had few or no rights under the law during the time of slavery, which also maintained their status as a racial minority, in terms of both their actual numbers and social standing in society. Minority groups include racial minorities, ethnic minorities, religious minorities, and others. Members of minority groups are frequently targets of discrimination precisely because they hold an identity other than that of the majority group in power. A recent Arizona law illustrates one of the concerns and controversies about laws that appear to single out minorities for unfair treatment.

In 2010, Arizona passed the controversial Support Our Law Enforcement and Safe Neighborhoods Act, otherwise known as Arizona Senate Bill 1070. The Arizona act made it a misdemeanor for noncitizens to be in Arizona without registration documents proving legal status. It also required Arizona law enforcement officers to check immigration status during the course of any lawful stop, detention, or arrest where "reasonable suspicion exists that the person is an alien and is unlawfully present in the United States." Individuals were presumed *not* to be illegal immigrants if they had a valid Arizona driver's or identification license, tribal identification, or government-issued identification. The Arizona act also directed local law enforcement to notify the United States Immigration and Customs Enforcement (ICE) or the United States Customs and Border Protection if it determined that an individual convicted of a violation of state or local law is in the country illegally. Even without conviction, the act encouraged law enforcement to transfer an illegal immigrant to federal custody.

Arizona's Support Our Law Enforcement and Safe Neighborhoods Act was a source of controversy the moment it was signed into law on April 23, 2010. In an April 2010 Gallup poll, 39 percent of Americans favored the Arizona law, 30 percent opposed it, and 31 percent had not heard of it or had no opinion. A day before it was to go into effect, a federal judge issued an injunction against the section that made it a state crime to fail to carry alien registration documents, the requirement that law enforcement officials check immigration status, and the component of the act that allowed a law enforcement officer to arrest a person without a warrant. The issue was taken to the US Supreme Court, which ruled, in June 2012, that state and local laws that direct law enforcement to investigate a person's immigration status are not unconstitutional. However, the Court also ruled that the criminalization of unlawful presence and the removal process is the duty of the federal government and may not be usurped by the state.

The part of the law that was left in place, the so-called show-me-your-papers provision, is very controversial. Some argue that directing law enforcement to check immigration status when there is "reasonable suspicion" amounts to racial profiling, subjecting those who look Mexican to more invasive police checks than those who do not appear to be from across the border. Garrett Epps wrote at *The American Prospect*, "Ethnic profiling is at the heart of 1070 and other state laws like it. Can 'driving while brown' be made a state crime?"[1] But Ilya Shapiro at *SCOTUSblog* claims, "Racial profiling is not at issue here. S.B. 1070 bends over backwards to make clear that it does not allow (let alone require) any use of race not permitted under federal law."[2] A poll of Latinos by the group Latino Decisions in 2012 after the Supreme Court's decision found

---

1. Garrett Epps, "Face It: SB 1070 Is About Race," *The American Prospect*, April 25, 2012. http://prospect.org/article/face-it-sb-1070-about-race.
2. Ilya Shapiro, "S.B. 1070: Constitutional but Bad Policy," *SCOTUSblog*, July 13, 2011. http://www.scotusblog.com/2011/07/s-b-1070-constitutional-but-bad-policy.

that 79 percent believe that Latinos in Arizona who are legal immigrants or US citizens will get stopped or questioned by police because of the act.

Like many laws affecting minorities, there is widespread disagreement about whether such laws intentionally and egregiously target minorities and, as such, are discriminatory. The viewpoints included in *At Issue: Minorities and the Law* illustrate that such controversy abounds regarding laws as varied as those affecting criminal justice, the minimum wage, voting rights, and affirmative action. The authors of these viewpoints take opposing views, providing a glimpse into some of the issues facing the United States today in enacting laws that impact minority groups.

1

Prison's Dilemma

Glenn C. Loury

Glenn C. Loury is the Merton P. Stoltz Professor of the Social Sciences at Brown University and author of The Anatomy of Racial Inequality.

The US imprisonment rate is extremely high and the majority of prisoners are minorities. Disparities in punishment rates are both a product of socioeconomic inequalities and a cause of them. The current penal regime amounts to a racial caste system. Although many blame poor, minority neighborhoods for creating young, male criminals, the reality is that society is partially responsible for the existence of these neighborhoods that breed these young, often black, male criminals who frequently end up in prison.

Over the past four decades, the United States has become a vastly punitive nation, without historical precedent or international parallel. With roughly 5 percent of the world's population, the U.S. currently confines about one-quarter of the world's prison inmates. In 2008, one in a hundred American adults was behind bars. Just what manner of people does our prison policy reveal us to be?

America, with great armies deployed abroad under a banner of freedom, nevertheless harbors the largest infrastructure for the mass deprivation of liberty on the planet. We imprison nearly as great a fraction of our population to a lifetime in jail (around seventy people for every hundred thousand residents) than Sweden, Denmark, and Norway imprison for any duration whatsoever.

That America's prisoners are mainly minorities, particularly African Americans, who come from the most disadvantaged corners of our unequal society, cannot be ignored. In 2006, one in nine black men between the ages of twenty and thirty-four was serving time. The role of race in this drama is subtle and important, and the racial breakdown is not incidental: prisons both reflect and exacerbate existing racial and class inequalities.

Why are there so many African Americans in prison? It is my belief that such racial disparity is not mainly due to overt discriminatory practices by the courts or the police. But that hardly exhausts the moral discussion. To begin with, let's remember the fact that the very definition of crime is socially constructed: as graphically illustrated by the so-called "war on drugs," much of what is criminal today was not criminal in the past and may not be tomorrow.

Let us also frankly admit that a massive, malign indifference to people of color is at work. I suspect strongly, though it is impossible to prove to the econometrician's satisfaction, that our criminal and penal policies would never have been allowed to expand to the extent that they have if most of the Americans being executed or locked away were white.

For people who go to prison, time behind bars almost always also diminishes their odds of living crime-free lives when they get out.

We must also frankly ask why so many African American men are committing crimes. Many of the "root causes" have long been acknowledged. Disorganized childhoods, inadequate educations, child abuse, limited employability, and delinquent peers are just a few of the factors involved. In America, criminal justice has become a second line of defense, if you will, against individuals whose development has been neglected or undermined by other societal institutions, like welfare, education, employment and job training, mental health programs, and other social initiatives. As a result, it is an arena in which social stratification, social stigmas, and uniquely American social and racial dramas are reinforced.

We should also remember that "punishment" and "inequality" are intimately linked—that causality runs in both directions. Disparities in punishment reflect socioeconomic inequalities, but they also help produce and reinforce them.

Is it not true, for example, that prisons create criminals? As the Rutgers criminologist Todd Clear concluded after a review of evidence, the ubiquity of the prison experience in some poor urban neighborhoods has had the effect of eliminating the stigma of serving time. On any given day, as many as one in five adult men in these neighborhoods is behind bars, and as Clear has written, "[T]he cycling of these young men through the prison system has become a central factor determining the social ecology of poor neighborhoods, where there is hardly a family without a son, an uncle or a father who has done time in prison."

For people who go to prison, time behind bars almost always also diminishes their odds of living crime-free lives when they get out, by lowering employability, severing ties to healthy communal supports, and hardening their own attitudes. When such individuals return to their communities, they join many others with the same harsh life experience, often forming or joining gangs. This, in turn, further diminishes the opportunities that law-abiding residents in those same neighborhoods have to escape poverty or preserve the (often meager) value of their property.

Huge racial disparities in the incidence of incarceration should therefore come as no surprise. The subordinate status of black ghetto-dwellers—their social deprivation and spatial isolation in America's cities—puts them at greater risk of embracing dysfunctional behaviors that lead to incarceration, and then incarceration itself leads to more dysfunction.

Put it all together and look at what we have wrought. We have established what looks to the entire world like a racial caste system that leaves millions stigmatized as pariahs, either living behind bars or in conditions of concentrated crime and poverty that breed still more criminality. Why are we doing this?

The present American regime of hyper-incarceration is said to be necessary in order to secure public safety. But this is not a compelling argument. It is easy to overestimate how much crime is prevented by locking away a large fraction of the population. Often those who are incarcerated, particularly for selling drugs, are simply replaced by others. There is no shortage of people vying to enter illicit trades, particularly given how few legal paths to upward mobility exist for most young black males.

The desperate and vile behaviors of some ghetto-dwellers reflect not merely their personal moral deviance, but also the shortcomings of our society as a whole.

The key empirical conclusion of the academic literature is that increasing the severity of punishment has little, if any, effect in deterring crime. But there is strong evidence that increasing the *certainty* of punishment has a large deterrent effect. One policy-relevant inference is that lengthy prison sentences, particularly in the form of mandatory minimum-type statutes such as California's Three Strikes Law, are difficult to justify.

The ideological justification for the present American prison system also ignores the fact that the broader society is implicated in the existence of these damaged, neglected, feared, and despised communities. People who live in these places are aware that outsiders view them with suspicion and contempt. (I know whereof I speak in this regard, because I am myself a child of the black ghetto, connected intimately to ghetto-dwellers by the bond of social and psychic affiliation. While in general I am not much given to advertising this fact, it seems appropriate to do so here.)

The plain historical truth of the matter is that neighborhoods like North Philadelphia, the West Side of Chicago, the East Side of Detroit, and South Central Los Angeles did not come into being by an accident of nature. As the sociologist Loïc Wacquant has argued, these ghettos are man-made, coming into existence and then persisting because the concentration of their residents in such urban enclaves serves the interests of others. As such, the desperate and vile behaviors of some ghetto-dwellers reflect not merely their personal moral deviance, but also the shortcomings of our society as a whole. "Justice" operates at multiple levels, both individual and social.

Defenders of the current regime put the onus on lawbreakers: "If they didn't do the crimes, they wouldn't have to do the time." Yet a pure ethic of personal responsibility does not and could never justify the current situation. Missing from such an argument is any acknowledgment of social responsibility—even for the wrongful acts freely chosen by individual persons.

I am not saying that a criminal has no agency in his behavior. Rather, I am arguing that the larger society is implicated in a criminal's choices because we have acquiesced to social arrangements that work to our benefit and to his detriment—that shape his consciousness and his sense of identity in a way that the choices he makes (and that we must condemn) are nevertheless compelling to him.

Put simply, the structure of our cities with their massive ghettos is a causal factor in the deviancy among those living there. Recognition of this fact has far-reaching implications for the conduct of public policy. What goals are our prisons trying to achieve, and how should we weigh the enormous costs they impose on our fellow, innocent citizens?

In short, we must think of justice as a complex feedback loop. The way in which we distribute justice—putting people in prison—has consequences, which raise more questions of justice, like how to deal with convicts' families and communities, who are also punished, though they themselves have done nothing wrong. Even if every sentence handed out to every prisoner were itself perfectly fair (an eminently dubious proposition), our system would still be amoral, because it punishes innocents. Those who claim on principled arguments that "a man deserves his punishment" are missing the larger picture. A million criminal cases, each rightly decided— each distributing justice to a man who deserves his sentence— still add up to a great and historic wrong.

2

The Criminal Justice System Is Not Unfair to Minorities

John Perazzo

John Perazzo is the managing editor of DiscoverTheNetworks.org and the author of The Myths That Divide Us: How Lies Have Poisoned American Race Relations.

The public's reaction to the killing of African American Trayvon Martin in Florida in February 2012, reflects the common perception that the criminal justice system in the United States is biased against racial minorities. In fact, multiple studies dispute this claim, finding that there is no racial bias at prosecution or sentencing, but that people of color are arrested more because they commit more crimes. The myth persists as a result of the efforts of American law schools and the civil-rights establishment.

Given the way the left has depicted Trayvon Martin's death [February 2012]—as a case of a "white Hispanic" who "hunted down" a young African American and was subsequently given a pass by a corrupt and racist criminal-justice system—one could hardly have been shocked to learn that on April 7th [2012] in Gainesville, Florida, a group of at least five black men shouted "Trayvon!" before proceeding to beat an innocent, 27-year-old white pedestrian so badly as to leave his face permanently disfigured. Neither was it particularly surprising when, four days later—again in Gainesville—a black crowd shouted "Trayvon!" while assaulting a white man who was trying to wrest his female companion's purse from the hands of a black man who had just stolen it. Nor could it be described as stunning that someone in Sanford, Florida shot six bullets into an empty police cruiser on the morning of April 10th—to register an unmistakable vote of disapproval over how local police had purportedly mishandled their response to George Zimmerman's recent killing of Martin.

A Perception of Bias

The foregoing actions were those of people seeking retribution for two very separate offenses. First, of course, there was the killing of Martin—an act which, according to a Gallup poll, 72% of blacks (as compared to 31% of non-blacks) view mainly a result of Zimmerman's own racial bias. Second, and much more important, was the perception that law-enforcement's decision not to incarcerate the gunman in the immediate aftermath of the shooting reflected a racial bias that pervades the entire criminal-justice system of the United States. Gallup reports that 73% of blacks (vs. 35% of non-blacks) believe that Zimmerman would have been arrested (and presumably jailed) if his victim had been white, while a new ABC poll finds that 84% of blacks feel that the justice system—from the police to the courtroom to the penitentiary—treats them inequitably.

A disproportionate number of blacks [are] in prison not because of a double standard of justice, but because of the disproportionate number of crimes they committed.

While it is virtually impossible to overstate the implications of this core belief which has so firmly embedded itself in the worldview of black Americans, one vital question begs for an answer: *Is it true?* Let us briefly survey the mountain of empirical evidence that the champions of "civil rights"—like [civil rights activists Jesse] Jackson and [Al] Sharpton—have so carefully avoided mentioning amid their incessant, thundering denunciations of the U.S. and its justice system.

The criminal-justice process is comprised of a number of stages, or decision points, at which law-enforcement personnel (such as police and judges) must determine how they should proceed—arrest or release a suspect; convict or acquit; impose a harsh or mild sentence; etc. Contrary to popular mythology, there is virtually no evidence of racial discrimination at any of these decision points. Black overrepresentation is almost entirely at the arrest stage, reflecting the simple fact that the "average" black engages in criminal activity more frequently than the "average" white. Not only are the outcomes at other decision points nearly identical for both races, but the slight differences that do exist tend to favor blacks. Further, the arrest rates of blacks living in cities that are ... politically black-controlled are no lower than the arrest rates of blacks in white-controlled cities. Nor are these realities anything new; they have been true for decades.

Consider that as early as 1983, the liberal-leaning National Academy of Sciences found "no evidence of a widespread systematic pattern of discrimination in sentencing." In 1985 the *Journal of Criminal Law and Criminology* concluded that a disproportionate number of blacks were in prison not because of a double standard of justice, but because of the disproportionate number of crimes they committed. That same year, federal government statistician Patrick Langan conducted an exhaustive study of black and white incarceration rates and found that "even if racism [in sentencing] exists, it might explain only a small part" of the black overrepresentation among prison inmates. In a 1987 review essay of the three most comprehensive books examining the role of race in the American criminal-justice system, the journal *Criminology* concluded that there was little evidence of anti-black discrimination. The most exhaustive, best-designed study of comparative sentencing patterns—a 1990 analysis of more than 11,000 recently convicted criminals in California—found that the severity of sentences depended heavily on such factors as prior criminal records, the seriousness of the crimes, and whether guns were used in the commission of those crimes; race was found to have no effect whatsoever. A 1991 RAND Corporation study found that a defendant's racial or ethnic background bore little or no relationship to conviction rates; far more important than race were such factors as the amount of evidence presented, and whether or not a credible eyewitness testified.

In 1993 a Justice Department study tracked the experience of more than 10,000 accused felons in America's 75 largest cities [and] found that black defendants fared better than their white counterparts—66% of black defendants were actually prosecuted, versus 69% of white defendants; among those prosecuted, 75% of blacks were convicted, as compared to 78% of whites. Similarly, a 1996 analysis of 55,000 big-city felony cases found that black defendants were convicted at a lower rate than whites in 12 of the 14 federally designated felony categories. This finding was consistent with the overwhelming consensus of other, previous, well-designed studies, most of which indicated that black defendants were slightly less likely to be convicted of criminal charges against them than white defendants. In 1997, liberal criminologists Robert Sampson and Janet Lauritsen conducted a painstaking review of the voluminous literature on charging and sentencing, and concluded that "large racial differences in criminal offending," and not racism, explained why proportionately more blacks than whites were in prison—and for longer terms.

A Manufactured Problem

The foregoing realities remain as true today as they were two and three decades ago. Even though a massive industry, devoted entirely to uncovering any trace evidence of bias in the justice system, has arisen in America's law schools and the civil-rights establishment, the net result of its cumulative efforts has been nothing more than an occasional study indicating a miniscule, unexplained racial disparity in sentencing, while most other analyses continue to find no racial effect at all.

Of course, one could never learn any of this from the "civil rights leaders" who were apparently struck mute in the aftermath of an April 3rd shooting that occurred outside a south Phoenix Taco Bell restaurant, where a 22-year-old black motorist at the drive-through window got into an altercation with Daniel Adkins, a 29-year-old, mentally disabled "white Hispanic" pedestrian. The argument grew heated, and the driver shot and killed Adkins. When police arrived at the scene, the gunman reported that Adkins had swung a bat or metal pipe at him. Though no such items were ever found at the scene, an independent witness reported that Adkins had swung his fists in the driver's direction several times. Arizona, like Florida, has a "Stand Your Ground" law that allows a person to use deadly force when faced with a life-or-death confrontation. The gunman accordingly claimed that he had acted in self-defense, and thus he was not arrested.

While Daniel Adkins' death was undeniably a human tragedy, it is quite conceivable that from a legal standpoint, the gunman, if in fact he felt that his life was in danger, acted within the bounds of the law. What is noteworthy, however, is that few Americans have ever heard of Daniel Adkins. Jackson and Sharpton have said nothing about him. Famous athletes and entertainers have not "tweeted" about him. And President [Barack] Obama has felt no compulsion to exhort his countrymen, as he did in the wake of the Trayvon Martin killing, "to do some soul-searching to figure out how does something like this happen." Now, why do you suppose that is?

3

The War on Marijuana in Black and White

American Civil Liberties Union

The American Civil Liberties Union (ACLU) is a national organization dedicated to defending and expanding all civil liberties and civil rights in America.

The war on drugs has always targeted poor communities of color, beginning with the enforcement of heroin and crack cocaine laws. In recent decades, however, that attention has shifted to the enforcement of marijuana laws, which has become a war on people of color, with wealthier whites using marijuana without fear of arrest. The best solution to remedy the costly and unjust enforcement of marijuana prohibition is to legalize it, or at the very least decriminalize the use of the drug.

Over the past 40 years, the United States has fought a losing domestic drug war that has cost one trillion dollars, resulted in over 40 million arrests, consumed law enforcement resources, been a key contributor to jaw-dropping rates of incarceration, damaged countless lives, and had a disproportionately devastating impact on communities of color. The ferocity with which the United States has waged this war, which has included dramatic increases in the length of prison sentences, and has resulted in a 53% increase in drug arrests, a 188% increase in the number of people arrested for marijuana offenses, and a 52% increase in the number of people in state prisons for drug offenses, between 1990 and 2010. Indeed, the United States now has an unprecedented and unparalleled incarceration rate: while it accounts for 5% of the world's population, it has 25% of the world's prison population.

The War on Drugs

Despite costing billions of dollars, the War on Drugs has polluted the nation's social and public health while failing to have any marked effect on the use or availability of drugs. Indeed, the United States is the world's largest consumer of illegal drugs. On the 40th anniversary of the War on Drugs, former President Jimmy Carter declared it a total failure, noting that global drug use for all drugs had increased in the years since the drug war started.

The first half of the War on Drugs focused largely on relentless enforcement of heroin and crack cocaine laws in poor communities of color. But with the ebb of the crack epidemic in the late 1980s, law enforcement agencies began shifting to an easy target: marijuana. As a result, over the past 20 years police departments across the country have directed greater resources toward the enforcement of marijuana laws. Indeed, even as overall drug arrests started to decline around 2006, marijuana arrests continued to rise, and now make up over half of all drug arrests in the United States. In 2010, there were more than 20,000 people incarcerated on the sole charge of marijuana possession.

In the states with the worst disparities, Blacks were on average over six times more likely to be arrested for marijuana possession than whites.

Stated simply, marijuana has become the drug of choice for state and local police departments nationwide. Between 2001 and 2010, there were 8,244,943 marijuana arrests, of which 7,295,880, or 88%, were for marijuana possession. In

2010 alone, there were 889,133 marijuana arrests—300,000 more than arrests for all violent crimes combined—or one every 37 seconds. There were 140,000 more marijuana arrests in 2010 than in 2001, and 784,021 of them, or 88%, were for possession.

A War on People of Color

The war on marijuana has largely been a war on people of color. Despite the fact that marijuana is used at comparable rates by whites and Blacks, state and local governments have aggressively enforced marijuana laws selectively against Black people and communities. In 2010, the Black arrest rate for marijuana possession was 716 per 100,000, while the white arrest rate was 192 per 100,000. Stated another way, a Black person was 3.73 times more likely to be arrested for marijuana possession than a white person—a disparity that increased 32.7% between 2001 and 2010. It is not surprising that the War on Marijuana, waged with far less fanfare than the earlier phases of the drug war, has gone largely, if not entirely, unnoticed by middle- and upper-class white communities.

In the states with the worst disparities, Blacks were on average over six times more likely to be arrested for marijuana possession than whites. In the worst offending counties across the country, Blacks were over 10, 15, even 30 times more likely to be arrested than white residents in the same county. These glaring racial disparities in marijuana arrests are not a northern or southern phenomenon, nor a rural or urban phenomenon, but rather a national one. The racial disparities are as staggering in the Midwest as in the Northeast, in large counties as in small, on city streets as on country roads, in counties with high median family incomes as in counties with low median family incomes. They exist regardless of whether Blacks make up 50% or 5% of a county's overall population. The racial disparities in marijuana arrest rates are ubiquitous; the differences can be found only in their degrees of severity.

Thus, while the criminal justice system casts a wide net over marijuana use and possession by Blacks, it has turned a comparatively blind eye to the same conduct occurring at the same rates in many white communities. Just as with the larger drug war, the War on Marijuana has, quite simply, served as a vehicle for police to target communities of color.

To the extent that the goal of these hundreds of thousands of arrests has been to curb the availability or consumption of marijuana, they have failed. In 2002, there were 14.5 million people aged 12 or older—6.2% of the total population—who had used marijuana in the previous month; by 2011, that number had increased to 18.1 million—7.0% of the total population. According to a World Health Organization survey of 17 countries, 42.2% of Americans have tried marijuana in their lifetime. The 2010 National Survey on Drug Use and Health reported similar numbers—39.26% of Americans surveyed reported having used marijuana in their lifetimes—and over 17.4 million Americans had used marijuana in the past month. Between 2009 and 2010, 30.4% of 18- to 25-year-olds reported having used marijuana at least once in the past month.

The Enforcement of Marijuana Laws

All wars are expensive, and this war has been no different. States spent over $3.61 billion combined enforcing marijuana possession laws in 2010. New York and California combined spent over $1 billion in total justice system expenditures just on enforcement of marijuana possession arrests. Had marijuana been regulated like alcohol, and had its use been treated as a public health issue akin to alcohol instead of as a criminal justice issue, this is money that cities, counties, and police departments could have invested in an array of other law enforcement priorities and community initiatives.

Marijuana arrests, prosecutions, and convictions have wrought havoc on both individuals and communities, not only causing direct harm but also resulting in dire collateral consequences. These include affecting eligibility for public housing and student financial aid, employment opportunities, child custody determinations, and immigration status. Marijuana convictions can also subject people to more severe charges and sentences if they are ever arrested for or convicted of another crime. In addition, the targeted enforcement of marijuana laws against people of color, and the unsettling, if not humiliating, experience such enforcement entails, creates community mistrust of the police, reduces police-community cooperation, and damages public safety.

We stand at a strange crossroads in America with regards to marijuana policy.

Concentrated enforcement of marijuana laws based on a person's race or community has not only been a central component of this country's broader assault on drugs and drug users, it has also resulted from shifts in policing strategies, and the incentives driving such strategies. Over the past 20 years, various policing models rooted in the "broken windows" theory, such as order-maintenance and zero-tolerance policing, have resulted in law enforcement pouring resources into targeted communities to enforce aggressively a wide array of low-level offenses, infractions, and ordinances through tenacious stop, frisk, and search practices. Indeed, it seems hard to avoid the conclusion that police tactics of effectuating a high volume of arrests for minor offenses has been a major contributor to the 51% rise in marijuana arrests between 1995 and 2010. Adding further stimuli to such policing strategies are COMPSTAT—a data-driven police management and performance assessment tool—and the Byrne Justice Assistance Grant Program, a federal funding mechanism used by state and local police to enforce drug laws. These programs appear to create incentives for police departments to generate high numbers of drug arrests, including high numbers of mari-juana arrests, to meet or exceed internal and external perfor-mance measures.

So we stand at a strange crossroads in America with re-gards to marijuana policy. On the one hand, as of November 2012, two states—Colorado and Washington—have legalized marijuana; 19 jurisdictions (18 states and the District of Columbia) allow marijuana for medical purposes; a majority of Americans favor both full legalization as well as legalizing marijuana for medicinal purposes; whites and Blacks use mari-juana at comparable rates, and many residents of middle- and upper-class white communities use marijuana without legal consequence or even fear of entanglement in the criminal jus-tice system. On the other hand, in 2010 there were over three-quarters of a million arrests for marijuana—accounting for al-most half of the almost 1.7 million drug arrests nationwide—for which many people were jailed and convicted. Worse yet, Blacks were arrested for marijuana possession at almost four times the rate as whites, with disparities even more severe in several states and counties, and the country spent billions of dollars enforcing marijuana laws.

In addition to ending marijuana possession arrests, police departments should reform order-maintenance policing strategies that focus on low-level offenses.

The Need for Marijuana Legalization

But the right road ahead for this country is clearly marked: marijuana possession arrests must end. In place of marijuana criminalization, and taking a cue from the failure of alcohol prohibition, states should legalize marijuana, by licensing and regulating marijuana production, distribution, and possession for persons 21 or older. Legalization would, first and foremost, eliminate the unfair race- and community-targeted enforcement of marijuana criminal laws; help reduce overincarceration in our jails and prisons; curtail infringement upon constitutional rights, most notably as guaranteed by the Fourth Amendment's proscription of unreasonable searches and seizures; and allow law enforcement to focus on serious crime.

Furthermore, at a time when states are facing budget shortfalls, legalizing marijuana makes fiscal sense. The licensing and taxation of marijuana will save states millions of dollars currently spent on enforcement of marijuana criminal laws. It will, in turn, raise millions more in revenue to reinvest in public schools and substance abuse prevention, as well as general funds and local budgets, research, and public health, to help build stronger, safer communities. Indeed, Washington State's Office of Financial Management projects that Initiative 502, which legalized the possession of marijuana for people 21 or older under tight regulations, will generate more than half a billion dollars in new revenue each year through a 25% marijuana excise tax, retail sales, and business and occupation taxes. The state will direct 40% of the new revenues toward the state general fund and local budgets and 60% toward education, health care, substance abuse prevention, and research. At the national level, a CATO Institute study estimated that federal drug expenditures on marijuana prohibition in 2008 were $3.4 billion, and that legalization would generate $8.7 billion in annual revenue.

If legalizing marijuana through taxation, licensing, and regulation is unobtainable, states should significantly reduce marijuana arrests by removing all criminal and civil penalties for authorized marijuana use and possession for persons 21 or older. Under depenalization, there would be no arrests, prosecutions, tickets, or fines for marijuana use or possession as long as such activity complies with existing regulations governing such activities. If depenalization is unobtainable, states should decriminalize marijuana possession for personal use by reclassifying all related criminal laws as civil offenses only, with a maximum penalty of a small fine.

In addition to ending marijuana possession arrests, police departments should reform order-maintenance policing strategies that focus on low-level offenses. Instead, law enforcement should address public health questions and safety concerns in ways that minimize the involvement of the criminal justice system by moving toward non-punitive, transparent, collaborative community- and problem-oriented policing strategies. These strategies should aim to serve, protect, and respect all communities. In addition, the federal government should end inclusion of marijuana possession arrests as a performance measure of law enforcement agencies' use of or application for federal funds, and redirect such funds currently designated to fight the War on Drugs toward drug treatment, research on treatment models and strategies, and public education.

4

The Policy of Stop-and-Frisk Targets Young Men of Color

Scott Stringer

Scott Stringer is the comptroller of New York City and previously served as the twenty-six borough president of Manhattan.

The increasing use of stop-and-frisk in New York City constitutes separate and unequal policing, while also being ineffective. Instead of creating fear and distrust of law enforcement among blacks and Latinos, the call-in approach should be used to build relationships of trust where community members help combat crime. In addition, there should be more transparency and accountability with respect to police stops to ensure that these stops are effective and not simply used to justify racial profiling.

In the aftermath of the Trayvon Martin killing [in Florida in February 2012], New York City Mayor Michael Bloomberg rightly and forcefully condemned the "Stand Your Ground" law in Florida that encouraged self-appointed crime-stopper George Zimmerman to shoot first and ask questions later. But there was another dynamic at play that night in Sanford [Florida]—namely, the presumption that young men of color are potential criminals who can be stopped in their tracks, no matter what they are doing.

The Growth in Stop-and-Frisk

New York is not Sanford, of course, and there is a world of difference between the vigilantism of George Zimmerman and

Scott Stringer, "Beyond Stop-and-Frisk: Toward Policing That Works," reprinted with permission from the April 23, 2012, issue of *The Nation*. For subscription information call 1-800-333-8536. Portions of each week's Nation magazine can be accessed at www.thenation.com.

the professional policing of the nation's biggest city. But we can no longer stand by while innocent young men of color are stopped for the crime of walking home or going to the store.

On Tuesday, April 24 [2012], I will proudly stand with Martin Luther King III, who is coming to New York City to talk about justice and civil rights in the age of stop-and-frisk. Last year, the NYPD [New York Police Department] made over 680,000 stops—an increase of over 600 percent since 2002. Eighty-seven percent of those stopped were black or Latino, in a city where those groups comprise 54 percent of the population. And in 99.9 percent of those stops, no gun was recovered.

The younger King's visit comes forty-five years after his father, Dr. Martin Luther King Jr., took to the pulpit at Riverside Church in Manhattan and declared, "A time comes when silence is betrayal," and that "the fierce urgency of now" required all Americans to demand an end to the Vietnam War.

The moral challenge we confront in New York City today has changed, but Dr. King's words continue to ring true. As currently practiced, stop-and-frisk represents a continuation of separate and unequal policing on the streets of New York—an affront to Dr. King's legacy and a continued impediment to effective policing in America's largest city.

There are ... many proven policing strategies that work with communities, not against them, to reduce gun violence.

Of course, the sacrifices of our women and men of the NYPD cannot be understated. In the past two decades, crime rates have plunged, contributing to a rebirth in the city's economy and attracting a million more people to the five boroughs. This trend has continued under Police Commissioner

Ray Kelly. But the dramatic growth in stop-and-frisk numbers has cast a troubling shadow on these statistics.

During a recent City Council hearing that discussed alternatives to stop-and-frisk, Commissioner Kelly said: "What I haven't heard is any solution to the violence problems in these communities—people are upset about being stopped, yet what is the answer?"

In fact, there are many good answers to that question, and many proven policing strategies that work with communities, not against them, to reduce gun violence.

But first, some background.

The Use of Street Stops

The use of street stops by police is not new, and when constitutionally deployed, they can be a critical public safety tool. The Supreme Court first outlined the legal justification for street stops in the 1968 case of *Terry v. Ohio*, holding that the Fourth Amendment permits police to stop an individual on the street if the officer has reasonable suspicion that the person has committed, is committing, or is about to commit a crime and that he or she "may be armed and presently dangerous."

In the years since Terry, most cities have added street stops to their arsenal of crime-fighting weapons. But no city has used street stops with such frequency as New York.

The fruits of this New York City dragnet would be dismissed as an abject failure if applied to any other government initiative: in 94 percent of stops, no arrest is made.

The policy as practiced in New York is also riddled with racial profiling. As the *New York Times* editorialized last year [2011], the numbers suggest that "hundreds of thousands of people, mostly minorities, have been stopped for no legitimate reason—or worse, because of the color of their skin."

As a result, in today's New York, white parents and parents of color have completely different conversations with their children about the police. White children are taught early that if they are lost or in trouble, they should find a police officer. In black and Latino families, the conversation has become one of extreme caution, if not outright fear, of keeping a bad situation from getting worse.

I have seen firsthand evidence of this during recent Sunday visits to black churches. In some cases, mothers bring their sons with them and they speak angrily—despairingly—about police stops that humiliated their children for no good reason. Stop-and-frisk is not reaping guns but rather a deep layer of distrust between police and communities of color. And that makes solving crime harder, not easier.

[The call-in approach] rests, crucially, on demonstrating that law enforcement respects the difference between the violent few and everybody else in a neighborhood.

The Call-In Approach

There are better ways to keep our neighborhoods safe and our city united, starting with the groundbreaking community-oriented reforms pioneered by John Jay College of Criminal Justice Professor David Kennedy, the author most recently of the acclaimed *Don't Shoot: One Man, a Street Fellowship, and the End of Violence in Inner-City America.*

Armed with the knowledge that a small number of criminals commit the majority of violent crimes in any neighborhood, Kennedy devised a system—the "call-in" approach—where gang members, drug dealers and other "bad actors" are summoned to a meeting with law enforcement, clergy, community leaders and social services organizations.

At that meeting, what Kennedy calls "the moral voice of the community"—local parents who have lost children to gun violence, ex-offenders who have gone straight and faith leaders—sets an unmistakable community standard against violence. Individuals are given a choice—either stop committing violent crimes now, or watch as we arrest not just you but every member of your crew. In addition to people who can help them get their lives back on track, law enforcement is there, promising a greatly elevated risk of serious penalties for committing violent crimes.

It is a multi-pronged, multi-agency approach designed to stop the cycle of violence in a community, to give young people a second chance, to build bridges. It rests, crucially, on demonstrating that law enforcement respects the difference between the violent few and everybody else in a neighborhood.

In Hempstead, Long Island, the approach shut a raging open-air drug market dating back to the early 1980s. Not only did violent crime plummet, drug arrests dropped from around 124 a year to sixteen.

In Chicago, Yale Law School Professsor Tracey Meares used the same approach to target high-risk parolees in two violence-soaked police districts. Recidivism plummeted, while homicide in the neighborhoods dropped almost 40 percent per month. In Boston, call-ins became an integral part of Operation Ceasefire, which drove down youth homicide 63 percent in two years.

The Rev. Jeffrey Brown of the Union Baptist Church in Boston, who has been on the front lines of gang violence in that city for years, told my office of Operation Ceasefire: "The reason it works is because the community takes an active part in the strategy. They are involved with law enforcement as partners."

Relationships of trust, instead of suspicion, are forged. Community members are no longer passive observers; they are active participants in helping to combat crime. The police are viewed as protectors and partners.

Strategies like the call-in approach instill a sense of legitimacy in law enforcement, or what experts like Tom Tyler at

New York University School of Law call procedural justice. If people think they are getting a fair shake and being treated with respect—even if the outcome is not necessarily good for them—they are more likely to respect authority. And when people respect authority and believe the police are there to help, all of us are safer.

All of these strategies will make the NYPD tougher on crime by being smarter on crime.

In recent years, more than fifty jurisdictions have used Kennedy's approach, forming the National Network for Safe Communities. New York should be one of them.

Other Needed Reforms

Piloting the call-in approach is just one of many reforms the NYPD should employ. In addition, the Department should use CompStat—its data-driven accountability model credited with contributing to steep declines in crime—to hold precinct commanders accountable for high numbers of suspicion-less stops. Instead of lauding commanders for high numbers of stops regardless of their efficacy, the NYPD should focus on the "hit rate" of stops that actually recover weapons to ensure that they are being constitutionally deployed.

Gun buy-back programs also remain an effective tool. Working with clergy throughout the city, NYPD buy-back programs have taken over 7,600 weapons off the streets since 2008. One buy-back held in Brooklyn last year netted 182 weapons, including fifty-eight semi-automatic handguns, one sawed-off shotgun, two assault rifles and seven loaded weapons. That's more than 20 percent of the guns brought in by stop-and-frisk last year, or the equivalent yield of about 150,000 stops.

All of these strategies will make the NYPD tougher on crime by being smarter on crime.

If Dr. King's "Dream" was to be judged by the content of your character rather than the color of your skin, the sad truth is that too many young men of color in New York and beyond continue to live a nightmare, never knowing whether a simple trip to the corner store will lead to an encounter with the police.

Today, we cannot afford to wait any longer for reform while thousands among us suffer suspicion-less stops. We should not wait for the next Trayvon Martin.

5

Stop-and-Frisk Protects Minorities

Michael Barone

Michael Barone is senior political analyst for the Washington Examiner, *coauthor of* The Almanac of American Politics, *and a contributor to* Fox News.

The opposition to the stop-and-frisk practices of law enforcement in New York City is misguided. Stopping and questioning young people, and sometimes frisking them, has resulted in lower crime in New York City since illegal guns are not taken on the streets as often. Although young black and Hispanic men are more likely to be stopped, there is nothing wrong with this as these groups commit more violent crimes and are more frequently the victims of violent crimes.

New York City seems on the verge of making the same mistake that Detroit made 40 years ago. The mistake is to abolish the NYPD practice referred to as stop-and-frisk. It's more accurately called stop, question, and frisk. People were stopped and questioned 4.4 million times between 2004 and 2012. But the large majority were not frisked.

The effectiveness of this police practice, initiated by Mayor Rudy Giuliani in 1994 and continued by Mayor Michael Bloomberg, is not in doubt. The number of homicides—the most accurately measured crime—in New York fell from a peak of 2,605 in 1990 to 952 in 2001, Giuliani's last year in office, to just 414 in 2012.

Nevertheless, the three leading Democratic mayoral candidates in the city's September primary all have pledged to end stop-and-frisk. And last week, federal judge Shira Scheindlin, in a lawsuit brought by 19 men who have been stopped and frisked, found that the practice is unconstitutional and racially discriminatory.

Bloomberg has promised to appeal, and several of Scheindlin's decisions in high-profile cases have been reversed. But the leading Democratic candidates for mayor promise, if elected, to drop the appeal. The two leading Republican candidates support stop-and-frisk, but their chances of election seem dim in a city that voted 81 percent for Barack Obama in 2012.

What riles opponents of stop-and-frisk is that a high proportion of those stopped are young black and Hispanic males. Many innocent people undoubtedly and understandably resent being subjected to this practice. No one likes to be frisked, including the thousands of airline passengers who are every day. But young black and, to a lesser extent, Hispanic males are far, far more likely than others to commit (and be victims of) violent crimes, as Bloomberg points out. I take no pleasure in reporting that fact and wish it weren't so.

Frequent stop-and-frisks combined with mandatory three-year sentences for illegal possession of a gun mean that bad guys in New York don't take them out on the street much.

This was recognized by, among others, Jesse Jackson, who in 1993 said, "There is nothing more painful for me at this stage in my life than to walk down the street and hear footsteps and start to think about robbery and then look around and see it's somebody white and feel relieved."

You can get an idea about what could happen in New York by comparing it with Chicago, where there were 532 homicides in 2012. That's more than in New York, even though New York's population is three times as large. One Chicagoan who supports stop-and-frisk is the father of Hadiya Pendleton, the 15-year-old girl shot down a week after singing at Barack Obama's second inauguration. "If it's already working, why take it away?" he told the *New York Post*. "If that was possible in Chicago, maybe our daughter would be alive."

Chicago and New York both have tough gun-control laws. But bad guys can easily get guns in both cities. The difference, as the *New York Daily News*'s James Warren has pointed out, is that frequent stop-and-frisks combined with mandatory three-year sentences for illegal possession of a gun mean that bad guys in New York don't take them out on the street much. Stop-and-frisk makes effective the otherwise ineffective gun control that Bloomberg so strongly supports.

An extreme case of what happens when a city ends stop-and-frisk is Detroit. Coleman Young, the city's first black mayor, did so immediately after winning the first of five elections in 1973. In short order Detroit became America's murder capital. Its population fell from 1.5 million to 1 million between 1970 and 1990. Crime has abated somewhat since the Young years, but the city's population fell to 713,000 in 2010—just over half what it was when Young took office.

People with jobs and families—first whites, then blacks—fled to the suburbs or farther afield. Those left were mostly poor, underemployed, in too many cases criminal—and not taxpayers. As a result, the city government went bankrupt last month.

New York has strengths Detroit always lacked. But it is not impervious to decline. After Mayor John Lindsay ended tough police practices, the city's population fell from 7.9 million in 1970 to 7.1 million in 1980.

Those who decry stop-and-frisk as racially discriminatory should remember who is hurt most by violent crime—law-abiding residents of high-crime neighborhoods, most of them black and Hispanic, people like Hadiya Pendleton.

6

Minimum-Wage Madness

Thomas Sowell

Thomas Sowell is the Rose and Milton Friedman Senior Fellow at the Hoover Institution of Stanford University.

There is currently a movement to raise the minimum wage in order to help the poor. Such a proposal is misguided: in fact, all minimum-wage laws are actually damaging, not helpful, to the poor. When wages are artificially inflated by legislation, there is higher unemployment. Evidence supports this correlation between low unemployment and the lack of a minimum wage. Minorities and young people are the most likely to be harmed by the minimum wage by being unable to find work.

Political crusades for raising the minimum wage are back again. Advocates of minimum-wage laws often give themselves credit for being more "compassionate" towards "the poor." But they seldom bother to check what are the actual consequences of such laws.

One of the simplest and most fundamental economic principles is that people tend to buy more of something when the price is lower and less when the price is higher. Yet advocates of minimum-wage laws seem to think that the government can raise the price of labor without reducing the amount of labor that will be hired.

When you turn from economic principles to hard facts, the case against minimum-wage laws is even stronger. Countries with minimum-wage laws almost invariably have higher rates of unemployment than countries without minimum-wage laws.

Most nations today have minimum-wage laws, but they have not always had them. Unemployment rates have been very much lower in places and times when there were no minimum-wage laws.

Switzerland is one of the few modern nations without a minimum-wage law. In 2003, *The Economist* magazine reported: "Switzerland's unemployment neared a five-year high of 3.9 percent in February." In February of this year, Switzerland's unemployment rate was 3.1 percent. A recent issue of *The Economist* reported Switzerland's unemployment rate as 2.1 percent.

Most Americans today have never seen unemployment rates that low. However, there was a time when there was no federal minimum-wage law in the United States. The last time was during the Coolidge administration, when the annual unemployment rate got as low as 1.8 percent. When Hong Kong was a British colony, it had no minimum-wage law. In 1991, its unemployment rate was under 2 percent.

As for being "compassionate" toward "the poor," this assumes that there is some enduring class of Americans who are poor in some meaningful sense, and that there is something compassionate about reducing their chances of getting a job.

When minimum-wage levels are set without regard to their initial productivity, young people are disproportionately unemployed—priced out of jobs.

Most Americans living below the government-set poverty line have a washer and/or dryer, as well as a computer. More than 80 percent have air conditioning. More than 80 percent also have both a landline and a cell phone. Nearly all have television and a refrigerator. Most Americans living below the official poverty line also own a motor vehicle and have more living space than the average European—not Europeans in poverty, the average European.

Why then are they called "poor"? Because government bureaucrats create the official definition of poverty, and they do so in ways that provide a political rationale for the welfare state—and, not incidentally, for the bureaucrats' own jobs.

Most people in the lower income brackets are not an enduring class. Most working people in the bottom 20 percent in income at a given time do not stay there over time. More of them end up in the top 20 percent than remain behind in the bottom 20 percent.

There is nothing mysterious about the fact that most people start off in entry-level jobs that pay much less than they will earn after they get some work experience. But when minimum-wage levels are set without regard to their initial productivity, young people are disproportionately unemployed—priced out of jobs.

In European welfare states where minimum wages, and mandated job benefits to be paid for by employers, are more generous than in the United States, unemployment rates for younger workers are often 20 percent or higher, even when there is no recession.

Unemployed young people lose not only the pay they could have earned but, at least equally important, the work experience that would enable them to earn higher rates of pay later on.

Minorities, like young people, can also be priced out of jobs. In the United States, the last year in which the black unemployment rate was lower than the white unemployment rate—1930—was also the last year when there was no federal minimum-wage law. Inflation in the 1940s raised the pay of even unskilled workers above the minimum wage set in 1938. Economically, it was the same as if there were no minimum-wage law by the late 1940s.

In 1948 the unemployment rate of black 16-year-old and 17-year-old males was 9.4 percent. This was a fraction of what it would become in even the most prosperous years from 1958 on, as the minimum wage was raised repeatedly to keep up with inflation.

Some "compassion" for "the poor"!

7

A Higher Minimum Wage Will Not Hurt Minorities or Eliminate Jobs

Richard Eskow

Richard Eskow is a senior fellow with the Campaign for America's Future and the host of The Zero Hour *on We Act Radio.*

The argument against raising the minimum wage is based on myths about minimum-wage workers and a skewed interpretation of data. Despite the claims that minimum-wage workers are often teenagers and minorities, the reality is that most minimum-wage workers are adults, many are parents, and the majority are women. There is no evidence that raising the minimum wage would lead to higher unemployment and no support for the view that the minimum wage is racist.

Corporate interests and their elected representatives have created a world of illusion in order to resist paying a decent wage to working Americans. They'd have us believe that minimum-wage workers are teens from '50s TV sitcoms working down at the local malt shoppe.

It's a retro-fantasy where corporate stinginess creates minority jobs, working parents can't possibly be impoverished, and nobody gets hurt except kids who drive dad's convertible and top up their allowances with a minimum-wage job slinging burgers.

But then, you probably need to resort to fantasy arguments when you're arguing against a minimum-wage increase supported by nearly three-quarters of the voting public. That's also why it's important to demand that Congress allow an up-or-down vote on the Fair Minimum Wage Act, which would raise it to $10.10 and then index it to inflation.

Here's the truth: Most minimum-wage workers are adults, the majority of them are women, and many are parents who are trying to raise their children on poverty wages.

The Facts About Minimum-Wage Workers

Minimum-wage workers are adults.

Nearly 80 percent of the workers who would be directly affected by a minimum wage increase are adults, as seen in an analysis by the National Women's Law Center. When you include those who would be indirectly affected that figure becomes more than 92 percent.

Less than 16 percent of workers who would be affected by President [Barack] Obama's minimum-wage proposal are teenagers.

This may not be a Leave It to Beaver *world, but there are plenty of real-life Eddie Haskells.*

Minimum-wage workers are parents.

Many of those workers are parents. More than seven million children—nearly one out of every 10 kids in the United States—have parents whose income would go up under a new minimum wage. When you count the parents whose wages would be indirectly affected, that rises to more than 11 million (or roughly one in six) children whose households would benefit from the increase.

Most minimum-wage workers are women.

That's not something the right wants to emphasize. Other than formally declaring itself "anti-woman," there's not much more the GOP [Republican party] can do to lose the female vote. It certainly doesn't want people to notice that this is one more policy that disproportionately harms women.

The Fantasy About Minimum-Wage Workers

This may not be a [TV Sitcom] *Leave It to Beaver* world, but there are plenty of real-life Eddie Haskells.

Remember Eddie, the unctuous and untrustworthy high-school self-promoter? Think [Republican presidential nominee in 2012] Mitt Romney—who supported raising the minimum wage, at least in principle, until he began a presidential campaign that was funded by his fellow millionaires and dependent on today's radical right. Then he reversed himself. . . .

Romney argued that the minimum wage should be tied, not to productivity or executive gains, but to world indicators. That would create a global wage race to the bottom, one that hurts everyone except the wealthiest corporate leaders worldwide. That's the point, of course.

Last month [March 2013] Republicans in Congress rejected a proposal that would have raised the minimum wage to $10.10. They've also indicated they would reject the president's more modest proposal for a $9.00 minimum.

True to form, they keep trotting out that tired old "malt shoppe" argument. Rep. Marsha Blackburn of Tennessee, for example, said she opposed a higher minimum wage because "you're going to exclude a lot of younger workers."

Remember, more than eight out of ten workers affected by a minimum wage hike are adults.

The Myths About the Minimum Wage

When it comes to the Right and the minimum wage, it's not all malted milks and sock hops. There's also their much-beloved fantasy of the minimum wage as "racist." Seriously. It's a dirty argument to make—but then, there's a lot of money at stake.

Roy Edroso is one of a hardy band of writers whose beat includes the ever-growing body of "right-wing lit." (We owe them a debt of gratitude. They go spelunking in the dark caves of the human spirit so that we don't have to.) Edroso points us to Jonah Goldberg's assertion that the minimum wage's original backers were racists who supported it specifically because it harms black people.

Bizarrely enough, this is a common right-wing stratagem. The *Wall Street Journal* even calls an increased minimum wage "The Minority Youth Unemployment Act." While it's touching to note the editors' new-found solicitude toward nonwhite kids, they're ignoring the fact that the vast majority of minimum-wage workers aren't "youth."

The right keeps projecting its liquid illusions onto the walls of their political reality like a low-rent psychedelic show.

They aren't *minorities*, either. Awkwardly enough for race-baiters like Goldberg and the *Journal*, most minimum-wage workers are white. There are more minorities among minimum-wage earners (who are 57.9 percent white) than in the overall workforce (which is 67.9 percent white). But that doesn't support the "race" arguments against raising the minimum wage.

The Effects of Raising the Minimum Wage

Neither do the economic analyses, unless you rely on the highly selective economic studies employed by the *Journal* and other anti-minimum-wage advocates. Some rely on "meta-studies," or analyses of earlier studies, which selectively pick and choose from earlier works. Others rely on the work of economists with a pronounced ideological bent to the right.

The short answer to their job-creation argument is this: The minimum wage has dropped 30 percent in real dollars since 1968. *Where are the jobs?*

Meanwhile, the right keeps projecting its liquid illusions onto the walls of their political reality like a low-rent psychedelic show in . . . well, in 1968, when the minimum wage was much higher and the economy was doing much better than it is today. (The official unemployment rate that year was 3.6 percent.)

Here's another mind-bending image: We're told that raising the minimum wage would harm small companies—but most low-wage employees work for large corporations.

We're also told that employers can't afford to raise their pay, but these corporations are experiencing record-level profits.

And so the debate rages on, fueled by the cheap hallucinogenic deceptions of the corporate-funded right. Corporate profits continue to soar. CEO [chief executive officer] pay keeps skyrocketing. Suburban skylines are being reshaped by the megamansions of our New Gilded Age.

And meanwhile the Real Faces of the Minimum Wage— the mothers, fathers, the young and the old—struggle to survive and raise their children in an increasingly harsh world, far from the media spotlight and invisible to the powerful interests arrayed against them.

8

Opposition to Voter ID Laws Is Insulting to Minorities

David Limbaugh

David Limbaugh is a columnist and author of The Great De-
stroyer: Barack Obama's War on the Republic.

*The opposition to voter identification laws is outrageous, as there
is nothing radical about requiring people to prove citizenship in
order to vote. There is a legitimate concern about voter fraud
and such identification (ID) laws are not racist. Opposing such
voter ID laws on the grounds that it harms minorities is pro-
foundly disrespectful to minorities by making the assumption
that minority voters are unable to furnish identification. Such
opposition is politically motivated and intended to increase
Democratic votes.*

This is a headline we should never see in the United States:
"Federal Judge: Yes, Arizona and Kansas Can Require Voters To Prove Their Citizenship."

The Controversy over Voter-ID Laws

The fact that this issue would be disputed at all is astonishing.
That it is legally contested is stunning. That the prime mover
in initiating the legal challenge is our own federal government, which has a compelling interest in ensuring the integrity of the election process, is mind-blowing.

David Limbaugh, "Opposing Voter ID Laws in the Name of Race Is Insulting to Minorities," *Human Events*, March 21, 2014. By permission of David Limbaugh and Creators
Syndicate, Inc.

Who would have imagined just a few short years ago that in 2014 the executive branch of the federal government and a good chunk of its legislative branch would be dominated by radical community organizers wreaking havoc on the rule of law and our cherished principles of equal protection under the law and the impartial administration of justice? I feel like I'm living inside some Red-conspiracy fiction novel that could never get published because it's too unlikely to survive the incredulity even of readers with a generous willingness to suspend disbelief.

Both Kansas and Arizona passed new voter-ID legislation requiring new voters to provide a birth certificate, a passport or other documentation to prove their citizenship. But the U.S. Election Assistance Commission rejected requests from these two states for help in changing federal election registration forms. The existing federal registration form doesn't require proof of citizenship, only that new voters sign a statement declaring their citizenship.

How do you think the Internal Revenue Service would respond if we all said it would have to take our word for our income and expenses based on our "declarations" and we were not going to furnish 1099s, W2s or expense receipts?

What would the NSA [National Security Agency] say if all airline passengers simply refused to show their driver's licenses at airport security checkpoints?

What we want is to make sure the election process is fair, that only people who are eligible to vote are allowed to vote and vote just once.

Is the integrity of our elections so unimportant to President [Barack] Obama, Attorney General [Eric] Holder and the rest of the Democratic cabal that they refuse to impose the slightest checks against voter fraud?

The Charge of Racism

Well, some horrendously naive people take these leftists at their word that they believe voter fraud is a "rare" phenomenon, even though 46 states have prosecuted cases of voter fraud since 2000. Do you think they don't know about the pernicious activities of ACORN [Association of Community Organizations for Reform Now], with which they were joined at the hip?

Some people also take Democrats at their word that they believe initiatives for voter-ID laws are being driven by "racist" conservatives who want to suppress minority turnout in elections. This, too, is maliciously twisted thinking, most likely born of liberal projection. Democrats need look no further than their own consistent efforts to suppress the military vote.

I know a lot of conservatives, and I've never met one who thinks this way. What we want is to make sure the election process is fair, that only people who are eligible to vote are allowed to vote and vote just once.

I wish more minorities would vote for Republican candidates, but neither I nor any other conservative or Republican I've ever met would support suppressing minority votes just because they vote disproportionately Democratic.

Guy Benson of *Townhall* reports that after Georgia implemented its voter-ID law in 2007, which was upheld in court, the state saw an increase in minority voter participation in the next two election cycles.

An Insult to Minorities

How could any intellectually honest person maintain that it is unfair, unreasonable or unconstitutional to require all voters to provide documentation to verify that they are who they say they are before being allowed to vote?

What you need to understand is that with this bunch of Democrats everything is about politics. For them, the end justifies any means, and their paramount end is to get Democrats elected, and so they will pursue it, even at the expense of the integrity of the system. This is undeniable given their opposition to voter-ID laws.

What other conclusion can we draw from their opposition than they want to increase Democratic votes with voters who abuse the election process?

Unless you have a very low opinion of minorities, how could you conceivably argue that it is racist to require that all voters prove their identity as a condition to voting? If anything racist is involved here, it is in the suggestion that minorities are too incompetent to furnish their IDs. How could you disrespect minorities any more that that?

If people can't muster their ID—I don't care who they are—then they don't deserve the privilege of voting, and people who want to protect their right to do so without ID are on their face suspect.

It is a crying shame that our federal government is run by partisan Democrats who are waging war against the integrity of the election process, the rule of law and the sovereignty of the several states. I pray more people wake up to this reality.

9

Voter ID Laws Disenfranchise Minority Voters

Jeremiah Goulka

Jeremiah Goulka writes about American politics and culture for various media outlets.

Republicans support the passage of voter identification laws purportedly to counteract fraud at the polls. However, the real intent appears to be a desire to keep those who are more likely to vote for Democratic candidates—the poor, minorities, and the young—from being able to vote. People who are black and poor are much less likely to have proper identification, and getting such identification can be costly and full of obstacles. If Republicans really wanted to further democracy, they would need to implement such laws along with changes that make it free and easy to obtain the required voter identification.

Democrats are frustrated: Why can't Republican voters see that Republicans pass voter ID laws to suppress voting, not fraud?

Democrats know who tends to lack ID. They know that the threat of in-person voter fraud is wildly exaggerated. Besides, Republican officials could hardly have been clearer about the real purpose behind these laws and courts keep striking them down as unconstitutional. Still, Republican support remains sky high, with only one third of Republicans recognizing that they are primarily intended to boost the GOP's [Republican party] prospects.

How can Republican voters go on believing that the latest wave of voter ID laws is about fraud and that it's the *opposition* to the laws that's being partisan?

To help frustrated non-Republicans, I offer up my own experience as a case study. I was a Republican for most of my life, and during those years I had no doubt that such laws were indeed truly about fraud. Please join me on a tour of my old outlook on voter ID laws and what caused it to change.

Dems would use any crooked tool in the box to steal elections. Therefore America needed cleaner elections, and cleaner elections meant voter ID laws.

The Concern About Fraud

I grew up in a wealthy Republican suburb of Chicago, where we worried about election fraud all the time. Showing our IDs at the polls seemed like a minor act of political rebellion against the legendary Democratic political machine that ran the city and county. "Vote early and often!" was the catchphrase we used for how that machine worked. Those were its instructions to its minions, we semi-jokingly believed, and it called up an image of mass in-person voter fraud.

We hated the "Democrat" machine, seeing it as inherently corrupt, and its power, we had no doubt, derived from fraud. When it wasn't bribing voters or destroying ballots, it was manipulating election laws—creating, for instance, a signature-collecting requirement so onerous that only a massive organization like itself could easily gather enough John Hancocks to put its candidates on the ballot.

Republicans with long memories still wonder if Richard Nixon lost Illinois—and the 1960 election—thanks to Chicago

Mayor Richard Daley's ability to make dead Republicans vote for John F. Kennedy. For us, any new report of voter fraud, wrapped in rumor and historical memory, just hammered home what we already knew: it was rampant in our county thanks to the machine.

And it wasn't just Chicago. We assumed that all cities were run by similarly corrupt Democratic organizations. As for stories of rural corruption and vote tampering? You can guess which party we blamed. Corruption, election fraud, and Democrats: they went hand-in-hand-in-hand.

Sure, we were aware of the occasional accusation of corruption against one or another Republican official. Normally, we assumed that such accusations were politically motivated. If they turned out to be true, then you were obviously talking about a "bad apple."

I must admit that I did occasionally wonder whether there were any Republican machines out there, and the more I heard about the dominating one in neighboring DuPage County, the less I wanted to know. (Ditto Florida in 2000.) Still, I knew—I *knew*—that the Dems would use any crooked tool in the box to steal elections. Therefore America needed cleaner elections, and cleaner elections meant voter ID laws.

Adults Who Lack ID

Every once in a while I'd hear the complaint—usually from a Democrat—that such laws were "racist." Racist? How could they be when they were so commonsensical? The complainers, I figured, were talking nonsense, just another instance of the tiresome PC [politically correct] brigade slapping the race card on the table for partisan advantage. If only they would scrap their tedious, tendentious identity and victim politics and come join the rest of us in the business of America.

All this held until one night in 2006. At the time, my roommate worked at a local bank branch, and that evening when we got into a conversation, he mentioned to me that the bank required two forms of identification to open an account. Of course, who wouldn't? But then he told me this crazy thing: customers would show up with only one ID or none at all—and it wasn't like they had left them at home.

"Really?" I said, blown away by the thought of it.

"Yeah, really."

And here was the kicker: every single one of them was black and poor. As I've written elsewhere, this was one of the moments that opened my eyes to a broader reality which, in the end, caused me to quit the Republican Party.

I had no idea. I had naturally assumed—to the extent that I even gave it a thought—that every adult had to have at least one ID. Like most everyone in my world, I've had two or three at any given time since the day I turned 16 and begged my parents to take me to the DMV [Department of Motor Vehicles].

Until then, I couldn't imagine how voter ID laws might be about anything but fraud. That no longer held up for the simple reason that, in the minds of Republican operators and voters alike, there is a pretty simple equation: Black + Poor = Democrat. And if that was the case, and the poor and black were more likely to lack IDs, then how could those laws *not* be aimed at them?

Whenever I tell people this story, most Republicans and some Democrats are shocked. Like me, they had no idea that there are significant numbers of adults out there who don't have IDs.

By definition, a law that intentionally imposes more burdens on minorities than on whites is racist, even if that imposition is indirect.

Of course, had I bothered to look, the information about this was hiding in plain sight. According to the respected Brennan Center for Justice at the New York University School of Law, 7% of the general voting public doesn't have an adequate photo ID, but those figures rise precipitously when you hit certain groups: 15% of voting age citizens making less than $35,000 a year, 18% of Americans over 65, and a full quarter of African Americans.

A recent study by other researchers focusing on the swing-state of Pennsylvania found that one in seven voters there lack an ID—one in three in Philadelphia—with minorities far more likely than whites to fall into this category. In fact, every study around notes this disparate demographic trend, even the low-number outlier study preferred by Hans van Spakovsky, the conservative Heritage Foundation's voter "integrity" activist: its authors still found that "registered voters without photo IDs tended to be female, African-American, and Democrat."

The Charge of Racism

The more I thought about it, the more I understood why Democrats claim that these laws are racist. By definition, a law that intentionally imposes more burdens on minorities than on whites is racist, even if that imposition is indirect. Seeing these laws as distant relatives of literacy tests and poll taxes no longer seemed so outrageous to me.

After I became a Democrat, I tried explaining this to some of the Republicans in my life, but I quickly saw that I had crossed an invisible tripwire. You see, if you ever want to get a Republican to stop listening to you, just say the "R" word: racism. In my Republican days, any time a Democrat started talking about how some Republican policy or act was racist, I rolled my eyes and thought Reagan-esquely, *there they go again.* . . .

We loathed identity politics, which we viewed as invidious—as well as harmful to minorities. And the "race card" was so simplistic, so partisan, so boring. Besides, what about all that reverse discrimination? Now *that* was racist.

We also hated any accusation that made it sound like we were personally racist. It's a big insult to call someone a racist or a bigot, and we loathed it when Democrats associated the rest of us Republicans with the bigots in the party. At least in my world, we rejected racism, which we defined (in what I now see as a conveniently narrow way) as intentional and mean-spirited acts or attitudes—like the laws passed by segregationist *Democrats*.

This will undoubtedly amaze non-Republicans, but given all of the above, Republican voters continue to hear the many remarkably blunt statements by those leading the Republican drive to pass voter ID laws not as racist but at the very worst *Democratist*. That includes comments like that of Pennsylvania House majority leader Mike Turzai who spoke of "voter ID, which is going to allow Governor [Mitt] Romney to win the state of Pennsylvania: done." Or state Representative Alan Clemmons, the principal sponsor of South Carolina's voter ID law, who handed out bags of peanuts with this note attached: "Stop Obama's nutty agenda and support voter ID."

Republican voters are ... blissfully ignorant of the real costs of getting an ID.

Besides, some would point out that these laws also affect other people like the elderly (who often vote Republican) or out-of-state college students (often white)—and the latter would make sense as a target, because in the words of New Hampshire House leader Bill O'Brien, that's the age when you tend to "foolishly ... do what kids do": "vote as a liberal." And yes, this might technically violate the general principle that clean elections should include everyone, but partisans won't mind the results.

This makes me wonder how bothered I would have been had I known how committed Republican strategists are to winning elections by shrinking the electorate rather than appealing to more of it. I did certainly harbor a quiet suspicion that, to the extent we were the party of the managerial class, we were inherently fated to be a minority party.

The Barriers to Getting ID

Another key reason why Republican voters see no problem with these laws is their big safety valve: if you don't have an ID, well, then, be responsible and go get one!

If, however, Republican voters are generally unaware of the high frequency of minorities, the poor, and the elderly lacking IDs, they are blissfully ignorant of the real costs of getting an ID. Yes, the ID itself is free for the indigent (to comport with the 24th Amendment's ban on poll taxes), but the documents one needs to get a photo ID aren't, and the prices haven't been reduced. Lost your naturalization certificate? That'll be $345. Don't have a birth certificate because you're black and were born in the segregated south? You have to go to court.

IDs would have to be truly free and easy to obtain. The poor should not be charged for the required documentation.

Similarly, Republican voters—and perhaps most others— tend not to be aware of how hard it can be to get an ID if you live in a state where DMV offices are far away or where they simply aren't open very often. One can only hope that would-be voters have access to a car or adequate public transportation, and a boss who won't mind if they take several hours off work to go get their ID, particularly if they live in, say, the third of Texas counties that have no ID-issuing offices at all.

I doubt that most Republican voters know that some Republican officials are taking steps to make it even harder to get that ID. Wisconsin Governor Scott Walker, to take an example, signed a strict voter ID law and then made a move to start closing DMV offices in areas full of Democrats, while increasing office hours in areas full of Republicans—this in a state in which half of blacks and Hispanics are estimated to lack a driver's license and a quarter of its DMV offices are open less than one day per month. (Sauk City's is open a whopping four times a year.) Somehow I doubt that this is primarily about saving money.

A Real Solution

One reason why voter ID laws are so politically successful is that they put Democrats in a weak position, forcing them to deny that in-person voter fraud exists or that it's a big deal. Republican voters and media simply won't buy that. It doesn't matter how many times the evidence of the so-called threat has been shown to be trumped up. It's a bad position to be in.

Providing examples of Republicans committing fraud themselves—whether in-person or, as in Massachusetts and Florida, with absentee ballots (a category curiously exempted from several of the Republican-inspired voter ID statutes)—won't provide a wake-up call either. Most Republican voters will shrug it off by saying, essentially, "everybody's doing it."

If we can't talk about race, and Republican voters insist that these laws really are about fraud, then maybe Democrats should consider a different tack and embrace them to the full—so long as they are redesigned to do no harm. IDs would have to be truly free and easy to obtain. The poor should not be charged for the required documentation. More DMVs should be opened, particularly in poor neighborhoods and rural areas, and all DMVs should have evening and weekend hours so that no one has to miss work to get an ID.

To be sure that the laws do no harm, how about mobile DMV units that could go straight to any area where people need IDs? Nursing homes, churches, senior centers, you name it. They could even register people to vote at the same time. Now that would be efficient—and democratic.

No, wait, I've got it: How about a mandatory ID card? Every American would receive a photo ID as soon as he or she turns 18. That's it! A national ID card!

Then voter ID laws would be the perfect thing, because we all want clean elections with high voter turnout, don't we?

Something tells me, though, that Republicans won't go for it.

10

The US Supreme Court Erred in Revising the Voting Rights Act

Andrew Cohen

Andrew Cohen is a contributing editor at The Atlantic, *a legal analyst for* 60 Minutes *and CBS Radio News, and a fellow at the Brennan Center for Justice at New York University School of Law.*

The US Supreme Court decision wrongly struck down several provisions of the Voting Rights Act that were meant to protect against racially discriminatory voting laws. The Court's decision will allow jurisdictions to impose restrictive new voting rules on minority citizens without having to get approval for such changes. The winners of the ruling are those in favor of racial redistricting and voter identification laws, whereas the losers are minorities, the poor, and the elderly. America has not reached the point where protection from racially discriminatory voting laws is unnecessary.

Let's be clear about what has just happened [June 25, 2013]. Five unelected, life-tenured men this morning declared that overt racial discrimination in the nation's voting practices is over and no longer needs all of the special federal protections it once did. They did so, without a trace of irony, by striking down as unconstitutionally outdated a key provision of a federal law that *this past election cycle alone* protected the franchise for tens of millions of minority citizens. And they did so on behalf of an unrepentant county in the Deep South whose officials complained about the curse of federal oversight even as they continued to this very day to enact and implement racially discriminatory voting laws.

The Voting Rights Act

In deciding *Shelby County v. Holder,* in striking down Section 4 of the Voting Rights Act, the five conservative justices of the United States Supreme Court, led by Chief Justice John Roberts, didn't just rescue one recalcitrant Alabama jurisdiction from the clutches of racial justice and universal enfranchisement. By voiding the legislative formula that determines which jurisdictions must get federal "preclearance" for changes to voting laws, today's ruling enables officials in virtually every Southern county, and in many other jurisdictions as well, to more conveniently impose restrictive new voting rules on minority citizens. And they will. That was the whole point of the lawsuit. . . .

A black voter in Shelby County [Alabama] today, as a result of this ruling, has a much grimmer "future" when it comes to voting rights than she did yesterday.

In a 5-4 ruling over liberal dissent, the Supreme Court today declared "accomplished" a "mission" that has become more, not less, dire in the four years since the justices last revisited the subject. They have done so by focusing on voter turnout, which surely has changed for the better in the past fifty years, and by ignoring the other ruses now widely employed to suppress minority votes. In so doing, the five federal judges responsible for this result, all appointed by Republican presidents, have made it materially easier for Republican lawmakers to hassle and harry and disenfranchise likely Democratic voters. And they have done so by claiming that the Congress didn't mean what it said when it renewed the act by landslide votes in 2006.

No statute is ever perfect. Perhaps Congress should indeed have updated the "coverage formula" of Section 4 when it last revisited the law. But there are plenty of imperfect laws kept afloat by courts, including this Court. What happened here is that the Court's conservatives were no longer willing to countenance the intrusion upon "state sovereignty" that Section 4 represented in the absence of what they considered to be "updated" justifications for federal oversight. To the majority, the fact that "minority candidates hold office at unprecedented levels," was more important than the fact that Section 4 was invoked more than 700 times between 1982 and 2006 to block racially discrimination voting measures.

The Decision of the Court

The opinion itself is as accessible as any you are likely to read. Writing for the Court, the Chief Justice declared that Congress simply failed to update the "coverage formula" of Section 4 to address the very successes that the Voting Rights Act [VRA] has brought to minority voting rights over the past 50 years. If Congress is to divide the states between "covered" and uncovered jurisdictions, the Chief Justice wrote, it bears a heavy burden under the Tenth Amendment and "must identify those jurisdictions to be singled out on a basis that makes sense in light of current conditions. It simply cannot rely on the past."

The Fifteenth Amendment, which decrees "that the right to vote shall not be denied or abridged on account of race or color," the Chief Justice wrote in a remarkable passage, "is not designed to punish for the past; its purpose is to ensure a better future." Yet the Court's ruling today directly contradicts that lofty premise. A black voter in Shelby County today, as a result of this ruling, has a much grimmer "future" when it comes to voting rights than she did yesterday. Without Section

4's formula, Section 5 is neutered, and without Section 5 that black voter in Shelby County will have to litigate for her rights herself after the discriminatory law has come into effect.

In a passionate dissent, Justice Ruth Bader Ginsburg immediately homed in on the extraordinarily aggressive nature of what the Court has just done. "The question this case presents," she wrote, "is who decides whether, as currently operative, Section 5 remains justifiable, this Court, or a Congress charged with the obligation to enforce the post-Civil War amendments 'by appropriate legislation.'" Until today, Justice Ginsburg wrote, the Court "had accorded Congress the full measure of respect its judgments should garner" in implementing that anti-discriminatory intent of the Fourteenth and Fifteenth Amendments. Until today.

> Proponents of racial redistricting, or voter identification laws that are really a poll tax, will find succor in today's ruling.

"The Court," Justice Ginsburg wrote, "makes no genuine attempt to engage with the massive legislative record that Congress assembled. Instead, it relies on increases in voter registration and turnout as if that were the whole story." And then she proceeded to outline the countless ways in which racial discrimination in voting practices is alive and well in Alabama and other jurisdictions covered by the law. "The sad irony of today's decision," she wrote, "lies in its utter failure to grasp why the VRA has proven effective." It has been effective, of course, because it has made it harder for vote suppressors to suppress the votes of minority citizens. No more and no less.

The Winners of the Ruling

We should also be clear today about who the winners and the losers are in the wake of this opinion. The primary winners are vote suppressors in those many jurisdictions covered by Section 5, the politicians, lobbyists and activists who have in the past few years endorsed and enacted restrictive new voting laws in dozens of states. The legal burden now will be shifted from these partisans to the people whose votes they seek to suppress. This will mean that discriminatory practices will occur with greater frequency than they have before. The Constitution, the Court declared, must be color-blind and may not discriminate between states even if it means being blind to the political realities of a nation still riven by racial divides.

The Voting Rights Act isn't outdated. Its vitality was amply demonstrated in the years before the 2006 renewal, and in the years since.

Even in those jurisdictions not covered by Section 5 of the Voting Rights Act, lawmakers will cite today's ruling to justify future restrictions on voting—and in that sense this is a national disaster and not just a regional one. Proponents of racial redistricting, or voter identification laws that are really a poll tax, will find succor in today's ruling. And that means we will see more of these measures and, as we do, the people most directly impacted by them will have fewer ways in which to fend them off. The deterrent effect of Section 4, alone, was enormous. As U.S. District Judge John Bates remarked last year in a case out of South Carolina, its mere presence has stopped lawmakers from pitching hundreds more dubious laws.

So the winners today are officials like Rep. Darryl Metcalfe, the Republican state senator from Pennsylvania, who defended his state's statutory effort to suppress votes in the 2012 election by dog-whistling that those registered voters too "lazy" to get new identification cards didn't merit a ballot. Rep. Alan Clemmons, a Republican state representative from South Carolina, also wins today. He's a politician from a Section 5 state that sought to restrict voting rights. He answered "Amen" to a constituent who had written that encouraging black voters to get voter identification cards would "be like a swarm of bees going after a watermelon." Also winning big as a result of *Shelby County?* The grandees of the current iteration of the "voter fraud" myth.

The Losers of the Ruling

Who loses today? Not just the tens of millions of minority voters whose ability to cast a ballot now may be more easily restricted by new voting laws. Not just the millions who now will be more vulnerable to redistricting plans that are patently discriminatory. But the poor, the elderly, and the ill of all races, men and women who have voted lawfully for years but who will not be able to find the money to pay for new identification cards, or take the time out of work to travel to state offices to get one, or have the health to make the journey to obtain identification they otherwise do not need. These people, everywhere, were the indirect beneficiaries of Section 5 of the Voting Rights Act. And today their right to vote is far less secure.

So the losers today are registered voters like Craig Debose, a Vietnam veteran and longtime resident of South Carolina. Last year, he traveled 11 hours by train to Washington to testify in a Section 5 lawsuit. He doesn't have a car, which is why he didn't have photo identification, which is why he was going to be disenfranchised by state lawmakers until the Voting Rights Act saved him (for at least the last election cycle, the South Carolina law is still on the books). Losing today, too, is Jacqueline Kane, an elderly woman in Pennsylvania who had voted lawfully without incident for decades but who would have been forced from her nursing home to get an identification card. All to prevent "voter fraud" no one can prove.

Losing today also are citizens of all races in Texas who work for a living but cannot afford to travel hundreds of miles to state licensing offices. They were spared last year by Section 5 when a federal court declared, among other things, that officials intentionally limited the hours of operation for offices available to issue new identification cards so as to preclude the working poor from getting there. "A law that forces poorer citizens to choose between their wages and their franchise unquestionably denies or abridges their right to vote," declared a federal court last year. Today's ruling in Washington stands for precisely the opposite proposition.

A Weakening of Rights

The Court's majority is wrong. Terribly wrong. The Voting Rights Act isn't outdated. Its vitality was amply demonstrated in the years before the 2006 renewal, and in the years since. What has become outdated is the patience of a certain political and legal constituency in this country that has decided for itself over the past few years that there now has been *enough* progress toward minority voting to justify the law's demise. To this constituency, it is *enough* that more blacks and Hispanics now vote or are elected to office. To them, Section 4's actual burdens on officials—petty little bureaucratic burdens when compared to the burden of losing one's right to vote—suddenly are burdens so unreasonable they cannot be constitutionally borne.

Today's decision is the legal sanctification of an ugly movement that has brought America a new generation of voter suppression laws. It is the culmination of an ideological dream of a young Reagan Administration official named John Roberts, who sought 30 years ago to block an earlier renewal of the law. It is the latest manifestation of America's unfortunate eagerness to declare itself the grand victor even when a fight is clearly not won. Indeed, as today's setback demonstrates, the nation's fight for voting rights will never be over because the effort to undermine these rights is ceaseless. Section 4 of the Voting Rights Act was so strong that it took 48 years and this dubious ruling to bring it down. But down it has come.

For these reasons and many more, the Supreme Court's decision in *Shelby County* is one of the worst in the history of the institution. As a matter of fact, and of law, it is indefensible. It will be viewed by future scholars on a par with the Court's odious *Dred Scott* [*v. Sandford*] and *Plessy* [*v. Ferguson*] decisions and other utterly lamentable expressions of judicial indifference to the ugly realities of racial life in America. And to those tens of millions of Americans whose voting rights were protected *last year* by Section 4, it is a direct slap in the face rendered by judges who today used the banner of "states rights" to undermine the most basic right any individual can have in a free society—the right to be able to vote free from racial discrimination employed by public officials.

The America described by the Chief Justice, the one in which "blatantly discriminatory evasions of federal decrees are rare," is an America which has never once existed and which obviously does not exist today. The America the rest of us see so clearly with our own eyes, the America in which officials all over are actively seeking to suppress black and Hispanic votes, is the one that tens of millions of the rest of us have to live with, at least for now, without the protections of Section 4 of the venerable law. When rights are weakened for some, they are weakened for all. We all are much weaker today in the wake of this ruling.

11

The US Supreme Court Was Correct to Revise the Voting Rights Act

Hans A. von Spakovsky

Hans A. von Spakovsky is manager of the Election Law Reform Initiative and senior legal fellow in the Edwin Meese III Center for Legal and Judicial Studies at the Heritage Foundation.

The US Supreme Court was correct to strike down several provisions of the Voting Rights Act that were enacted in 1965 to protect against racially discriminatory voting laws. There is no evidence of widespread discrimination in certain parts of the country—as existed in 1965—that justifies continued meddling by the federal government in state voting laws. In fact, the provisions have in recent years been used for racial gerrymandering of districts. America has reached the point where extensive protection from racially discriminatory voting laws is unnecessary and current law is sufficient.

The Voting Rights Act [VRA] is one of the most important statutes ever passed by Congress to guarantee the right to vote free of discrimination. After the U.S. Supreme Court's correct decision in *Shelby County* [*v. Holder* (2013)], the VRA remains a powerful statute whose remedies are more than sufficient to protect all Americans. Both the Justice Department and private parties have the ability to stop those rare instances

Hans A. von Spakovsky, Testimony Before the Committee on the Judiciary, Subcommittee on the Constitution, US House of Representatives, Heritage Foundation, July 18, 2013. Copyright © 2013 by Heritage Foundation. All rights reserved. Reproduced by permission.

of voting discrimination when they occur using the various provisions of the VRA that protect individual citizens when they register and vote.

Prior to joining the Heritage Foundation, I was a Commissioner on the Federal Election Commission for two years. Before that I spent four years at the Department of Justice as a career civil service lawyer in the Civil Rights Division. I started as a trial attorney and was promoted to be Counsel to the Assistant Attorney General for Civil Rights, where I helped coordinate the enforcement of federal voting rights laws, including the Voting Rights Act and the National Voter Registration Act. I was privileged to be involved in dozens of cases on behalf of Americans of all backgrounds to enforce their right to register and vote in our elections.

The Need for Extraordinary Measures

As the Supreme Court said in its decision, "history did not end in 1965." Section 5 was originally passed as a temporary, emergency provision set to expire after five years. It was instead renewed four times, including in 2006 for an additional 25 years.

> *The systematic, widespread discrimination against black voters has long since disappeared.*

Section 5 was an unprecedented, extraordinary intrusion into state sovereignty since it required covered states to get the approval of the federal government for voting changes made by state and local officials—either the Department of Justice or a three-judge court in the District of Columbia. No other federal law presumes that states cannot govern themselves as their legislatures decide and must have the federal government's consent before they act. As the Supreme Court said, Section 5 "employed extraordinary measures to address an extraordinary problem."

Section 5 was necessary in 1965 because of the widespread, official discrimination that prevented black Americans from registering and voting as well as the constant attempts by local jurisdictions to evade federal court decrees. The disfranchisement rate was so bad that only 27.4 percent of blacks were registered in Georgia in 1964 and only 6.7 percent in Mississippi, compared to white registration of 62.6 percent and 69.9 percent, respectively. That disparity between black and white registration (and turnout) was a direct result of the horrendous discrimination suffered by black residents of those states.

The coverage formula of Section 4 was based on that disparity and Congress specifically designed it to capture those states that were engaging in such blatant discrimination. Thus, coverage under Section 4 was based on a jurisdiction maintaining a test or device as a prerequisite to voting as of Nov. 1, 1964, and registration or turnout of less than 50 percent in the 1964 election. Registration or turnout of less than 50 percent in the 1968 and 1972 elections was added in successive renewals of the law. That was the last time the coverage formula was revised, and Section 4 did not employ more current information on registration and turnout when Section 5 was last renewed in 2006.

Section 5 was needed in 1965. But as the Court recognized, time has not stood still and "[n]early 50 year later, things have changed dramatically." The systematic, widespread discrimination against black voters has long since disappeared. As the Court recognized in the *Northwest Austin* [*Municipal Utility District Number One v. Holder*] case in 2009: "Voter turnout and registration rates now approach parity. Blatantly discriminatory evasions of federal decrees are rare. And minority candidates hold office at unprecedented levels."

Evidence of Discrimination

As an example, in Georgia and Mississippi, which had such high disenfranchisement rates in 1964, black registration actually exceeded white registration in the 2004 election, just two years before Congress was considering the renewal of Section 5. Black registration exceeded white registration by 0.7 percent in Georgia and by 3.8 percent in Mississippi. The Census Bureau's May 2013 report on the 2012 election showed that blacks voted at a higher rate than whites nationally (66.2 percent vs. 64.1 percent).

That same report shows that based on Census regional data, black voting rates exceeded those of whites in Virginia, South Carolina, Georgia, Alabama, and Mississippi, which were covered in whole by Section 5, and in North Carolina and Florida, portions of which were covered by Section 5. Louisiana and Texas, which were also covered by Section 5, showed no statistically significant disparity between black and white turnout. Minority registration and turnout are consistently higher in the formerly covered jurisdictions than in the rest of the nation.

Without evidence of widespread voting disparities among the states, continuing the coverage formula unchanged in 2006 was irrational.

No one can rationally claim that there is still widespread, official discrimination in any of the covered states, or that there are any marked differences between states such as Georgia, which was covered, and states such as Massachusetts, which was not covered (except that Massachusetts has worse turnout of its minority citizens). As the Supreme Court approvingly noted and as Judge Stephen F. Williams pointed out in his dissent in the District of Columbia Court of Appeals, jurisdictions covered under Section 4 have "*higher* black registration and turnout" than noncovered jurisdictions. Covered jurisdictions also "have *far more* black officeholders as a proportion of the black population than do uncovered ones." In a study that looked at lawsuits filed under Section 2 of the VRA,

Judge Williams found that the "five worst uncovered jurisdictions ... have worse records than eight of the covered jurisdictions."

Arizona and Alaska, which were covered under Section 5, had not had a successful Section 2 lawsuit ever filed against them in the 24 years reviewed by the study. The increased number of current black officeholders is additional assurance that official, systemic discriminatory actions are highly unlikely to recur.

Without evidence of widespread voting disparities among the states, continuing the coverage formula unchanged in 2006 was irrational. As the Court said in the *Shelby County* decision, Congress "did not use the record it compiled to shape a coverage formula grounded in current conditions." Instead, it reenacted Section 4 "based on 40-year-old facts having no logical relation to the present day." It was no different than if Congress in 1965 had based the coverage formula not on what had happened in the prior year's election in 1964, but had instead opted to base coverage on registration and turnout from the Hoover era in 1928 or the Roosevelt election in 1932.

Section 5 was also unprecedented in the way it violated fundamental American principles of due process: it shifted the burden of proof of wrongdoing from the government to the covered jurisdiction. Unlike all other federal statutes that require the government to prove a violation of federal law, covered jurisdictions were put in the position of having to prove a negative—that a voting change was not intentionally discriminatory or did not have a discriminatory effect. While such a reversal of basic due process may have been constitutional given the extraordinary circumstances present in 1965, it cannot be justified today.

Congress also made another fatal mistake when it *expanded* the prohibitions in Section 5 in 2006. The Supreme Court had warned Congress that broadening Section 5 coverage would "exacerbate the substantial federalism costs that the preclearance procedure already exacts, perhaps to the extent of raising concerns about § [Section] 5's constitutionality." As the Court said in *Shelby County*, "the bar that covered jurisdictions must clear has been raised even as the conditions justifying that requirement have dramatically improved."

The Civil Rights Division of the Justice Department has abused its authority and power under Section 5 on numerous occasions.

Concerns About Section 5

Finally, two other serious problems must be noted with how Section 5 was interpreted and enforced. First, the "effects" test of Section 5 has led to a virtual apartheid system of redistricting, causing race to become a predominant factor in redistricting in covered jurisdictions. Jurisdictions are often forced to engage in racial discrimination to meet the Section 5 standard and create majority-minority districts. Rather than helping eliminate racial discrimination in voting, Section 5 has perpetuated it in redistricting and provided a legal excuse for legislators of both parties to engage in such discriminatory behavior when drawing boundary lines, manipulating district lines and isolating particular voters based entirely on their race. This is the exact opposite of the intention of the VRA, which the Supreme Court said was to "encourage the transition to a society where race no longer matters: a society where integration and color-blindness are not just qualities to be proud of, but are simple facts of life."

Second, the Civil Rights Division of the Justice Department has abused its authority and power under Section 5 on numerous occasions. South Carolina was forced to spend $3.5 million in 2012 litigating a specious objection filed by the Division against its voter ID law. A federal court found that there was no basis for the objection.

Similarly, during the Clinton administration, the American taxpayers were forced to pay over $4.1 million in attorneys' fees and costs awarded to defendants falsely accused of discrimination by the Division, including in several Section 5 cases.

For example, in *Johnson v. Miller*, which involved Georgia's 1992 legislative redistricting plan, a federal court severely criticized the Division for its unprofessional relationship with the ACLU [American Civil Liberties Union], the "professed amnesia" of its lawyers when questioned by the court over their activities (which the court found "less then credible"), and the Division's "implicit commands" to the Georgia legislature over how to conduct its redistricting. This case cost American taxpayers almost $600,000 in attorneys' fees and costs awarded to Georgia.

The district court found that the "considerable influence of ACLU advocacy on the voting rights decisions of the United States Attorney General is an embarrassment." The court was surprised that the Justice Department "was so blind to this impropriety, especially in a role as sensitive as that of preserving the fundamental right to vote." As the U.S. Supreme Court found, instead of basing its decision on Georgia's redistricting plan on whether there was evidence of discrimination as required under Section 5, "it would appear the Government was driven by its policy of maximizing majority-black districts."

In related cases filed in the early 1990s, a federal district court similarly criticized the Division, finding that it was trying to use its power "as a sword to implement forcibly its own redistricting policies." The court found that the Louisiana legislature "succumbed to the illegitimate preclearance demands of the Justice Department" that "impermissibly encouraged— nay, mandated—racial gerrymandering." Those cases cost the American public $1.1 million in attorneys' fees and costs awarded to Louisiana.

In 2012, the Division sent a legally preposterous letter to Florida claiming that the state government was violating Section 5 because it had not precleared the state's removal of noncitizens who had unlawfully registered to vote (five Florida counties are covered under Section 5). This despite the fact that noncitizens commit a federal felony when they illegally register to vote. As the *Federal Prosecution of Election Offenses* manual for federal prosecutors, published by the Criminal Division of the Justice Department, explains on pages 67–69, submitting false citizenship information in order to register to vote violates 18 U.S.C. §§ 1051(f) and 911.

The other provisions of the VRA are more than adequate to provide the Justice Department and private parties with the tools they need to go after discrimination on those infrequent occasions when it does still occur.

The Supreme Court's decision in *Shelby County* was correct under the facts, the law, and our Constitution. Section 5 was needed in 1965—it is not needed today and the coverage formula of Section 4 no longer reflects current conditions. Treating different states differently can no longer be justified.

The Need for Congressional Action

The question now becomes whether Congress should take any actions as a result of this decision. The answer to that question is "no." The other provisions of the VRA are more than adequate to provide the Justice Department and private parties with the tools they need to go after discrimination on those infrequent occasions when it does still occur.

The "heart" of the VRA today is Section 2, not Section 5. Section 2 applies nationwide, not just in a limited number of states and counties, and it is permanent; it will never expire. It forbids any "standard, practice, or procedure" that "results in a denial or abridgement of the right of any citizen of the United

States to vote on account of race or color" or membership in a language minority. Discriminatory measures or actions can be stopped before an election through temporary restraining orders and injunctions. Private plaintiffs can have their attorneys' fees and costs reimbursed if they are the prevailing party. Section 2 was not at issue in the *Shelby County* case and the Supreme Court's decision "in no way affects the permanent, nationwide ban on racial discrimination in voting found in §2."

The point here is that the Supreme Court in Shelby County *found that the general conditions in covered states today do not justify their continued exception from general constitutional principles and strictures.*

Section 2 is an effective remedy when it is utilized by the Civil Rights Division of the Justice Department. During the eight years of the [George W.] Bush administration, the Division filed 17 Section 2 lawsuits and obtained one out-of-court settlement. The current administration has barely utilized Section 2, having filed only one lawsuit since it came into office, and that suit was actually the outcome of an investigation started during the Bush administration. A recent report by the Inspector General of the Justice Department concluded that the "statistical evidence did not support" the claim that the Bush administration was hostile to Section 2 cases, particularly in light of the fact that the number of cases brought during the Bush administration far exceeded the number of cases brought during the current administration. The decreasing number of Section 2 cases may be an indication that discrimination is abating, further demonstrating that enforcement through Section 5 is not essential, or even necessary.

In order to meet the requirements of the Constitution, to justify federal supervision, a new Section 5 would have to identify those jurisdictions for which Section 2, because of systemic racial discrimination, would not be effective. That will not be possible because there is no evidence of systemic racial discrimination in voting in the states formerly covered under Section 4.

The lack of Section 5 enforcement does not mean jurisdictions can never be overseen by federal authorities. Another provision of the VRA, Section 3, can be used to supervise any jurisdictions that have a pattern of racial discrimination in voting. While the Supreme Court struck down the coverage formula of Section 4, Section 3 was not an issue in *Shelby County*. Section 3 has rarely been used, but it allows both for federal examiners and prior approval of voting changes.

If a jurisdiction has engaged in repeated discrimination and a court finds it is necessary to prevent future discrimination, Section 3 provides that the court can essentially place the jurisdiction into the equivalent of Section 5 coverage. Under a Section 3 finding, "no voting qualification or prerequisite to voting, or standard, practice, or procedure with respect to voting different from that in force or effect at the time the proceeding was commenced shall be enforced unless" the court or the Attorney General has precleared the change and found that it "does not have the purpose and will not have the effect of denying or abridging the right to vote." This preclearance thus becomes a tool to remedy discrimination that has been proven in court, rather than Section 5's blanket burden on all jurisdictions, regardless of their actual history and actions.

A Justified Decision

The point here is that the Supreme Court in *Shelby County* found that the general conditions in covered states today do not justify their continued exception from general constitutional principles and strictures. However, a court can still appoint federal examiners and place a particular jurisdiction into the equivalent of Section 5 preclearance if it finds sufficient evidence of current discrimination under Section 3's requirements. Also, unlike the due process problems inherent in Section 5, Section 3 does not shift the burden of proof for preclearance to covered jurisdictions *until* the government or a private plaintiff has *proven* that the jurisdiction has engaged in discrimination.

The VRA has other provisions that also remain in force to protect voters. This includes Section 11, which prohibits anyone from intimidating, threatening, or coercing any person for voting or attempting to vote. Sections 203 and 4(f)(4) require certain jurisdictions to provide bilingual registration and voting materials, including ballots, as well as interpreters and translators.

The Supreme Court correctly found that the coverage formula of Section 4 does not reflect current conditions and is therefore unconstitutional. As the Court concluded, "there is no valid reason to insulate the coverage formula from review merely because it was previously enacted 40 years ago." If Congress had first considered it in 2006, "it plainly could not have enacted the present coverage formula" because it "would have been irrational for Congress to distinguish between States in such a fundamental way based on 40-year-old data, when today's statistics tell an entirely different story."

The other provisions of the VRA such as Section 2 and Section 3 provide strong federal provisions to remedy voting discrimination if and when it occurs. My discussion of the robust provisions of the VRA that guarantee the right to vote does not even include the many other protections for voters that exist outside of the VRA in the National Voter Registration Act, the Uniformed and Overseas Citizens Absentee Voting Act, and the Help America Voting Act.

There is no reason for Congress to take any action to reinstate the coverage formula of Section 4. There is, in fact, no evidence that particular states are engaged in systematic discrimination that would justify treating them differently from other states.

12

Where Do Americans Stand on Affirmative Action?

Jamelle Bouie

Jamelle Bouie is a staff writer for Slate.

American opinion on affirmative action depends on how the question is worded. When couched just in terms of "considering race" there is less support, whereas when it is put in terms of "counteracting discrimination" there is more support. The majority of all races disfavor the former whereas only the majority of whites disfavor the latter. Whites believe that minorities get an unfair advantage with affirmative action when, actually, it is a policy that is still needed to counteract historical racial disparities.

The last week or so has seen several polls on the popularity of affirmative action, as a preface (of sorts) to the Supreme Court's anticipated ruling in *Fisher v. University of Texas*. But major differences between the polls make it difficult to judge where Americans stand on racial preferences.

One survey from *The Washington Post* and ABC News, for example, found a huge, diverse majority against "allowing universities to consider applicants race as a factor in deciding which students to admit."

Overall, 76 percent of Americans opposed race conscious admissions, while only 22 percent gave their support. This was consistent among all racial groups: 79 percent of whites opposed using race as a factor, along with 68 percent of Hispanics and *78 percent* of blacks. For opponents of affirmative action, this seems to be a welcome sign that the whole of American society has turned against race-based efforts to increase diversity in higher education.

But that's only one poll. Another survey, from NBC News and *The Wall Street Journal,* found a less decisive public. When asked if affirmative action programs were "still needed to counteract the effects of discrimination against minorities, and are a good idea as long as there are no rigid quotas," 45 percent of Americans agreed. On the other end, 55 percent of Americans supported the claim that "Affirmative action programs have gone too far in favoring minorities, and should be ended because they unfairly discriminate against whites."

Here, there's a much greater racial divide. Only 34 percent of whites agreed with the first statement, compared to 82 percent of African Americans and 68 percent of Latinos. By contrast, whites largely favored the second statement, with 56 percent affirming the view that whites are unfairly discriminated against in American life. These results are similar to an earlier poll from the Public Religion Research Institute, which finds 57 percent opposed to affirmative action in college admissions, with whites forming the bulk of opposition, and minorities broadly supportive.

Despite our short historical distance from Jim Crow . . . a majority of whites oppose any effort to increase diversity in college admissions.

Indeed, it's worth noting an even earlier poll from PRRI—released last spring—where 56 percent of white millennials said that government paid too much attention to the problems of minorities, and 58 percent said that discrimination against whites was "as big a problem as discrimination against blacks and other minorities."

All of this raises a question: What's up with *The Washington Post* results? No where else do we see such wide opposition to racial preferences in college admissions.

The answer is in the *wording* of *The Washington Post* poll. The *Post* doesn't ask if respondents are opposed to affirmative action—a policy which, for the most part, people understand, even if they are mistaken about its results—it asks if they support universities using "race as a factor." That's ambiguous. Does the *Post* mean affirmative action, or does it mean active discrimination against minority groups? There's a good chance that when confronted with the question, minority respondents reached for the second meaning, not the first. And obviously, blacks and Latinos are going to oppose anything that could block their path to upward mobility.

By explicitly asking about affirmative action and not just alluding to it, PRRI and *The Wall Street Journal* drew answers that line up with what we know about public opinion. Despite our short historical distance from Jim Crow—and the enduring legacy of economic and social policies meant to cement white supremacy—a majority of whites oppose any effort to increase diversity in college admissions. A majority of minorities, on the other hand, do not.

The "American public" isn't opposed to affirmative action—whites are. And while opposition is couched in terms of fairness, meritocracy, and colorblindness, there's also an element of resistance—many whites feel that minorities are getting an unfair advantage.

That they're getting an advantage isn't untrue. There are almost certainly cases of white students losing admission to elite schools (and otherwise) due to racial preferences. But, if we're serious about accounting for the past, that's unavoidable. For most of this country's history, all levels of government were used to advantage whites over all other racial groups, and blacks in particular. Whites were intentionally protected from competition in jobs, housing, education, and other areas of life. When you consider this, the call for complete meritocracy in college admissions is perverse—it does nothing but perpetuate existing disparities, which are large and growing.

This summer is the 50th anniversary of the March on Washington, and Martin Luther King Jr.'s "I Have a Dream" speech. As it approaches, a wide variety of public figures will affirm their commitment to King's dream of racial equality. Make no mistake—this is progress. But it also carries a whiff of insincerity. If we were fully committed to King's dream—if we truly aimed to fulfill his legacy—we would do far more to address the particular problems that face African Americans and other nonwhites, from mass incarceration and the war on drugs, to hyper-segregation and entrenched, generational poverty.

As a country, we invested a tremendous amount of time and energy into building a caste society of racial inequality, and we've taken huge strides in dismantling it. But to build a society of racial equality and opportunity takes even more time, and even more energy. Which is why I can't help but feel dread as we wait for the Supreme Court to announce its decisions on affirmative action and the Voting Rights Act. It's clear that a majority of the Court is willing to end the former and sharply limit the latter. And if it does, it's another sign that, regardless of what we say, we aren't prepared to do what it takes to secure genuine racial equality. We never have been, and likely, we never will be.

13

Do Race Preferences Help Students?

Richard Sander and Stuart Taylor Jr.

Richard Sander, a law professor at the University of California, Los Angeles (UCLA), and Stuart Taylor Jr., a nonresident senior fellow at the Brookings Institution, are authors of Mismatch: How Affirmative Action Hurts Students It's Intended to Help, and Why Universities Won't Admit It.

Research studying the use of racial preferences in university admissions reveals that when students are admitted to a college using racial preferences when they are only marginally qualified in comparison to other students, they perform worse than their peers who attend a college for which they qualify without preferences. There needs to be more transparency in university admissions to ensure that racial preferences are not harming the very students that they are supposed to help.

Affirmative action, long one of America's most divisive social issues, is about to grab headlines again. On Wednesday [October 10, 2012], the U.S. Supreme Court will hear arguments in a challenge to a state university's use of race in selecting students.

In many ways, the legal issues in *Fisher v. University of Texas* are the same as those that came before the court in 1978 and 2003. But the broader affirmative action debate has changed since those cases were heard, and in ways that could point toward compromises that might win broad public support.

Since the late 1960s, the racial preference discussion has been dominated by fairness questions. Proponents saw preferences as a necessary way of ensuring that racial minorities enjoy equal opportunity in the real world and not just paper promises of fair treatment. Opponents saw preferences as reverse discrimination, perpetuating racist habits under a new guise. But in recent years, scholars have started to do careful empirical research on whether preferences actually help their intended recipients. When the dispute shifts from "is it fair?" to "does it work?"—thus changing the focus from ideology to evidence—open-minded people can make progress toward consensus.

Much of this new research is on the idea of "mismatch"—on what happens after a student is admitted to a school for which he or she is only marginally qualified. (It is common for colleges to accept black applicants with SAT [college admission exam] scores several hundred points below those generally required for Asian or white applicants.) In general, however, studies have found that students tend to learn less if they are surrounded by peers with much stronger academic preparation.

Race is such a sensitive subject on most campuses, and diversity via racial preferences is viewed as so sacred, that campus presidents will often embrace even the flimsiest rebuttals of peer-reviewed, carefully replicated mismatch research.

Some 40% of black students entering college, for example, say they expect to major in science or engineering. But when they get to schools where most of the other students are better prepared—with much higher SAT scores and more rigorous high school course work—the chance of failure is high. Although some racial preference recipients rise to the challenge and perform better than ever, research finds that most tend to be overwhelmed and move to easier majors.

These are serious concerns. A raft of recent studies has found that students often fail to thrive if they are admitted to colleges for which they're far less prepared than their fellow students, and this holds true whether the preferences under which they were admitted were based on race (as are most very large preferences) or any other factor. Students admitted to schools under such programs are 30% to 40% less likely to get science degrees; they are twice as likely to fail the bar exam after law school; and they are likely to have less social interaction across racial lines.

These numbers are not comparing preference recipients with their better-qualified peers; they are comparing preference students with otherwise similar students who go to very good but less elite schools where they are better matched.

The mismatch hypothesis is controversial. The U.S. Commission on Civil Rights has issued two meticulously researched and reasoned reports expressing great concern about mismatch problems, but university leaders utterly ignored the reports, and they reject the idea of mismatch out of hand. Race is such a sensitive subject on most campuses, and diversity via racial preferences is viewed as so sacred, that campus presidents will often embrace even the flimsiest rebuttals of peer-reviewed, carefully replicated mismatch research.

In our view, the evidence is overwhelming that mismatches often harm those they are trying to help. Many skeptics are simply resisting serious scrutiny of current practices on political or emotional grounds. Others legitimately point out that there are important questions that need closer study, such as whether academic support can offset the effect of preferences, or whether the long-term advantages of an elite degree can offset mismatch troubles during college.

But even if the current evidence is viewed as inconclusive, there's an easy step the Supreme Court should consider: mandating transparency in university admissions systems that have long been cloaked in secrecy. Current court doctrine requires that preferences not be harmful to any racial group. Nearly all experts agree that Justice Anthony M. Kennedy is likely to write the decisive opinion in *Fisher,* and that he will be interested in putting more teeth into the court's high-sounding but so far unenforced principles curbing abuse of preferences. A great way to do this would be a simple consumer protection measure, requiring that when a college or university uses a racial preference, it provide applicants and admitted students with information about the outcomes of students whose qualifications are similar to theirs.

In many realms, it is taken for granted that consumers need good information: Home mortgages, cars and even cereal boxes come with extensive disclosures. It is hard to think of a major investment—especially one of such crucial lifelong importance—in which the consumers (students and their families) have so little information available about what exactly they are getting. Universities are ranked by outlets like *U.S. News & World Report* according to their prestige. But there is little information available that measures how schools actually serve their students.

In particular, those admitted with far lower scores or grades than the majority of students at the school need to know whether—and by how much—attending a more elite school is likely to hurt their grades and class rank. They should be able to gauge their chances of sticking with a tough major, graduating and passing licensing exams. Under current practices, there is simply no way to tell how students' qualifications on entry affect their academic success, and so students are left to rely on those alluring national rankings.

Requiring disclosures and transparency would empower students to make intelligent choices while still permitting colleges—at least for now—to continue offering large racial preferences. If the data tend to confirm that mismatched students fare poorly, then at least some students will shun preferences that are likely to land them out of their depth, and universities will probably work harder than they do now to provide effective academic support to struggling students. It would serve both skeptics and defenders of preferences to have the information needed to determine when, and how well, preference policies actually work.

14

The Next Affirmative Action

Kevin Carey

Kevin Carey is the director of the Education Policy program at the New America Foundation.

Affirmative action is on its way out because the US Supreme Court does not see the need for preferences to help minority students and because affirmative action has strayed far from its original purpose. Affirmative action should be used to level the playing field for students denied a chance at success, but too often the policy is only used to admit minority students to college without addressing the root causes of the problem, which include failing K-12 schools, a lack of support for completing college, and fair funding for colleges that serve minorities.

Affirmative action as we know it is dying. A growing number of states have moved to prohibit public universities from considering race in admissions, and the U.S. Supreme Court recently heard arguments in an anti-affirmative action lawsuit that left little doubt about where the Court's conservative majority stands. Less than a decade after the Court upheld racial admissions preferences in *Grutter v. Bollinger*, newer jurists like Samuel Alito and Chief Justice John Roberts seem ready to render unconstitutional a policy that has helped generations of minority students grab a rung on the ladder of opportunity.

Kevin Carey, "The Next Affirmative Action," *Washington Monthly*, vol. 45, no. 1/2, January/February 2013, pp. 55–57.

The Court's likely decision is particularly odious given the college admissions apparatus it will leave in place. Elite colleges warp and corrupt the meritocratic admissions process in a wide variety of ways. Academically substandard athletes, for example, are allowed in so they can play for the amusement of alumni and help shore up the fund-raising base. While some men's football and basketball players come from low-income and minority households, many athletes at the highly selective colleges where affirmative action really matters engage in sports like crew and lacrosse that are associated with white, privileged backgrounds. Colleges also give preference to the children of legacies, professors, celebrities, politicians, and people who write large checks to the general fund. All of these groups are also disproportionately wealthy and white.

In other words, the Supreme Court is poised to uphold affirmative action for everyone except minority students. We've come to this point in part because the Court has been packed with people like Roberts, who once struck down a plan to integrate public schools on the grounds that he saw no distinction between race-conscious policies that increased integration and the kind of brutal discrimination outlawed by *Brown v. Board of Education*. Apparently, John Roberts doesn't see race, so neither should anyone else.

It's time to return affirmative action to its original purpose: leveling the college playing field for students who have been unjustly denied a fair chance at success.

But affirmative action is also dying because it has strayed far from its original purpose. The justification for affirmative action the Court used in *Grutter* is that schools have a compelling interest in increasing racial diversity because students benefit from learning among people from disparate backgrounds. Affirmative action, once a pillar of the nation's work on behalf of the historically oppressed, is now allowable only on the grounds that it's good for white people.

This allowed Roberts to harangue lawyers defending the University of Texas's affirmative action policies by asking them how much diversity, exactly, they were shooting for, knowing that any specific answer could be struck down as an illegal quota. Perpetual swing vote and de facto King of America Anthony Kennedy, meanwhile, made the sensible critique that UT was giving preference to wealthy minority students, since the university presumably gets more than enough of the poor kind through a state law granting automatic admission to students who graduate in the top 10 percent of their high school class.

Regardless of how the Court ultimately rules, it's time to return affirmative action to its original purpose: leveling the college playing field for students who have been unjustly denied a fair chance at success. And the most important part of that project is expanding this idea far beyond elite colleges and universities.

While *Brown* is the iconic twentieth-century decision on race and educational justice, the 1954 decision was presaged by a number of crucial legal actions in higher education. Unsurprisingly, states with racist elementary and secondary school policies also discriminated against black students in their universities. In 1950, future Supreme Court Justice Thurgood Marshall argued and won *Sweatt v. Painter*, which prohibited UT from forcing black students into a separate law school.

And like *Brown*, the promise of those early victories has been substantially unfulfilled. More than half a century after states were instructed to desegregate with "all deliberate speed," the Justice Department still maintains a division of lawyers tasked with monitoring racial discrimination in public schools. (A DOJ headline from November 2012: "Justice Department Reaches Settlement with Georgia School District to Ensure All

Students Can Enroll in and Attend School.") And while public schools are no longer officially segregated, they are still governed by thousands of independent school districts that are substantially funded by local property taxes. Long-term residential and economic trends have made many of those districts impoverished and racially homogenous. As a result, minority students go to schools that on average receive less funding than those serving predominantly white students and are more likely to be staffed by unqualified teachers.

The same patterns persist in higher education. But here's where the two parts of our education system sharply diverge. Both K-12 and higher education continue to suffer from a legacy of racism. There is enormous awareness of the elementary and secondary side of the problem. George W. Bush's signature domestic policy achievement, the No Child Left Behind Act, was designed to erase the "achievement gap" between white and minority students, while the Obama administration's Race to the Top school initiative was touted by both candidates in the recent presidential debates. There is currently a roiling national argument about K-12 school reform, with partisans and advocates arguing for and against standardized testing, charter schools, teacher merit pay, school closings, and many other policies aimed at fixing low-performing schools.

Nationwide, the majority of all black and Latino college students fail to graduate within six years.

People may vehemently disagree about how to help minority students in K-12 education, but nearly all agree that the students need help in the first place. Yet in every big city with a headline-making, underperforming school district, there's a public higher education system receiving not 1/100th of the scrutiny. Detroit, for example, is widely seen to have the worst public school system in America—so bad that U.S. Secretary of Education Arne Duncan has said he "lose[s] sleep over" the plight of the city's 50,000 students. But how many people know that Wayne State, Detroit's main public university, has an 8 percent—yes, 8 percent—graduation rate for black students? Who's losing sleep over them?

Detroit is, no surprise, a worst case. But it's hardly the only city with a pervasive and largely ignored higher education problem. In Duncan's hometown, 19 percent of black students who enroll full-time at Chicago State University graduate within six years. At California State University, Los Angeles, it's 22 percent. The University of the District of Columbia matches Wayne State for futility, with an 8 percent graduation rate for black students. The University of Wisconsin-Milwaukee? 19 percent.

Texas Southern University in Houston was once the Texas State University for Negroes—the separate, unequal institution that the state created to avoid integration, leading to *Sweatt*. Today, it hosts the Thurgood Marshall School of Law and graduates 12 percent of its black undergraduates on time.

Nationwide, the majority of all black and Latino college students fail to graduate within six years. Even those who do finish may not be getting much benefit. Richard Arum and Josipa Roksa's blockbuster 2011 study *Academically Adrift*, which found "limited or no learning" taking place among a substantial percentage of all college graduates, also found significant racial disparities, with black students learning less than their white peers. Studies of literacy among college graduates have found similar patterns. Black students are also more likely than other groups to default on student loans that cannot be discharged in bankruptcy, leaving financial ruin in their wake, and minority students are targeted by for-profit colleges peddling sketchy degrees and inflated student loans. State governments, meanwhile, give far more money per student to flagship universities enrolling a disproportionately white, wealthy student body than to the regional universities and community colleges where most minority students are educated.

America's higher education system is comprehensively failing to give minority students what they need, and this has little to do with elite college admissions. Including community colleges, fewer than one in ten undergraduates attend colleges with admissions rates below 50 percent. By definition, affirmative action only affects the small percentage of students who are qualified to attend elite schools. Many of the minority students washing out of public universities in droves are the survivors of our infamously substandard K-12 schools, attending local, open-admissions institutions. Their problem isn't getting into college—it's getting out with a quality degree in hand and no terrible loans on their backs.

Those who set the national education agenda need to look past the handful of universities that graduate the ruling class and focus on improving the neglected institutions that educate future minority school teachers, scientists, doctors, and engineers.

So the end of affirmative action, absurd though it is, may be an opportunity to change the way people think about race and higher education. Affirmative action is one of a relatively small number of high-profile issues, like climate change, school vouchers, and abortion, that people form strongly held opinions about based largely on broad ideological affiliation. To be liberal is to favor admissions preferences in college; to be conservative is to oppose them. That's a powerful dynamic, but it has also had the effect of training generations of progressives to believe that they're doing their part to further the cause of racial justice in college by supporting affirmative action—and nothing else.

In reality, minority students need a much broader reform agenda, one that focuses on giving the colleges they attend a fair share of public resources and then holding them accountable for results. Not all colleges that enroll large numbers of black students have catastrophic graduation rates. Some, like Elizabeth City State University, a historically black public institution in North Carolina, get nearly half of their students through on time. Like many minority-serving institutions, Elizabeth City enrolls students whose academic preparation reflects the dysfunction of our K-12 schools. That's a tough job, and a university with real academic standards shouldn't necessarily let 100 percent of students earn a degree. But there's a huge difference between 8 percent and 50 percent, and the things universities like ECSU do to help students graduate aren't revolutionary: they bring new students to campus over the summer to help them acclimate, they carefully track their academic progress to look for warning signs of dropping out, and they focus hard on academics. But many unsuccessful colleges don't do these things—or don't do them well—because nobody outside the institution is paying attention.

States need to start practicing financial affirmative action by devoting more public resources to colleges that enroll students with the greatest academic needs. Along with the federal government, they should also penalize institutions with terrible graduation rates, student loan repayment rates, and post-graduation employment and earning rates, compared to peers with similar student populations. Those who set the national education agenda need to look past the handful of universities that graduate the ruling class and focus on improving the neglected institutions that educate future minority school teachers, scientists, doctors, and engineers. It will require the work of generations, but that's what minority college students— blinkered jurists notwithstanding—truly need.

15

Affirmative Action Should Be Based on Hardship Not Race

Ben Carson

Ben Carson is a columnist, retired neurosurgeon, and author of
One Nation: What We Can All Do to Save America's Future.

Affirmative action in university admissions was created to take into consideration the difficulties minorities face in a racist society and it has worked for many minority students. Today, many people of all races could use the extra consideration provided by affirmative action to take into account economic and other hardship. This compassionate action should not be limited to race, but should focus on giving credit to young people for overcoming obstacles, in order to help them succeed.

As a child growing up in Detroit and Boston, I had many opportunities to experience the ugly face of racism and witnessed the devastating toll exacted by its mean-spirited nature.

Minorities in a Racist Society

I was a victim of the racism of low expectations for black children, but in retrospect, I can see that many of those attitudes were based on ignorance. Large numbers of white people actually believed that blacks were intellectually inferior, and there was a host of other inaccurate beliefs that whites held about blacks and that blacks held about whites.

Ben Carson, "Beyond Affirmative Action," Townhall, February 19, 2014. By permission of Ben Carson and Creators Syndicate, Inc.

Many of those misperceptions probably would have persisted if measures had not been taken to abolish the separation of the races. One of those measures was affirmative action, which was based on the admirable concept that we should take into consideration inherent difficulties faced by minorities growing up in a racist society.

I believe that I benefited from affirmative action. When I applied to Yale University, I thought my chances of being accepted were favorable only because I was somewhat naive about admissions requirements for a high-powered Ivy League institution.

I graduated third in my high school class rather than at the top, largely because my sophomore year was a total waste after I got caught up in the negative aspects of peer pressure and abandoned my studies for the sake of social acceptance. I had a healthy grade-point average by the time I graduated, and one of the Detroit newspapers printed an article that stated I had the highest SAT [college admission exam] scores of any student graduating from the Detroit public schools in 20 years. I was also the city executive officer for the ROTC [Army Reserve Officers' Training Corps] program and had a long list of extracurricular activities.

I don't believe race determines underdog status today. Rather, it is the circumstances of one's life that should be considered.

The Benefits of Affirmative Action

In my mind, I was pretty hot stuff. Only after I got to Yale and became cognizant of my classmates' many accomplishments did I realize that the admissions committee had taken a substantial risk on me and that I had been extended special consideration. My early academic experiences were traumatic, and but for the grace of God, I would have flunked out.

Fortunately, I was able to adjust to the academic rigors necessary to qualify for medical school admission at the University of Michigan. Medical school was transformative, and I was subsequently accepted into the selective neurosurgical residency at Johns Hopkins. By that time, no special considerations were expected or needed.

Today, there are many young people from a variety of racial backgrounds who are severely deprived economically and could benefit from the extension of a helping hand in education, employment and other endeavors. Such extra consideration is actually helpful to all of us as a society. For each individual we prevent from going down the path of underachievement, there is one less person who will need support from governmental entitlement programs. More importantly, there is one more person who may make substantial contributions that benefit mankind.

The Need for Compassionate Action

The real question is this: Who should receive extra consideration from a nation that has a tradition of cheering for the underdog? My answer to that question may surprise many, but I don't believe race determines underdog status today. Rather, it is the circumstances of one's life that should be considered.

For example, let's take a child who is a member of a racial minority with parents who are successful professionals who have given their child every imaginable advantage. The child applies to a prestigious university with a 3.95 grade-point average, excellent SAT scores and a great record of community service. This child would obviously be an excellent candidate for admission.

Let's take another child who is white, but whose father is incarcerated and whose mother is an alcoholic. Despite these disadvantages, the child still has a 3.7 grade-point average, very good SAT scores and a resume that includes several low-paying jobs. Without taking any other factors into consideration, the choice is clear: The first student would be admitted over the second.

However, I think extra consideration should go to the second child, who has clearly demonstrated the tenacity and determination to succeed in the face of daunting odds. If that second child happens to be a member of a racial minority, obviously he would receive the extra consideration, as well.

I call this "compassionate action." Such a strategy demonstrates sensitivity and compassion, as well as recognition of substantial achievement in the face of difficult obstacles. The groups who benefit from compassionate action will probably change over time, depending on which ones have the greatest number of obstacles to overcome. The point is, it's time to be more concerned about the content of character than the color of skin when extending extra consideration.

Some people are still willfully ignorant and wish to look at external physical characteristics in determining a person's abilities. These people are unlikely to change even when equipped with information, because they already think they possess superior knowledge and wisdom. All we can do is pray that someday, they will have a change of heart.

Organizations to Contact

The editors have compiled the following list of organizations concerned with the issues debated in this book. The descriptions are derived from materials provided by the organizations. All have publications or information available for interested readers. The list was compiled on the date of publication of the present volume; names, addresses, phone and fax numbers, and e-mail and Internet addresses may change. Be aware that many organizations take several weeks or longer to respond to inquiries, so allow as much time as possible.

American Civil Liberties Union (ACLU)

125 Broad St., 18th Floor, New York, NY   10004
(212) 549-2500
website: www.aclu.org

The American Civil Liberties Union is a national organization that works to defend Americans' civil rights as guaranteed in the US Constitution. The ACLU Immigrants' Rights Project is dedicated to expanding and enforcing the civil liberties and civil rights of noncitizens and to combating public and private discrimination against immigrants. The ACLU publishes the semiannual newsletter *Civil Liberties Alert* as well as briefing papers and other publications, including "Immigration Myths and Facts."

American-Arab Anti-Discrimination Committee (ADC)

1990 M St. NW, Suite 610, Washington, DC   20036
(202) 244-2990 • fax: (202) 333-3980
e-mail: adc@adc.org
website: www.adc.org

The American-Arab Anti-Discrimination Committee is a civil rights organization committed to defending the civil rights of people of Arab descent. ADC has full-time attorneys in its legal department and works with the government to promote the interests of the community. It publishes a series of issue papers and a number of books, including "Arab and Muslim Civil Rights and Identity: A Selection of Scholarly Writings from the Decade After 9/11."

Amnesty International USA

5 Penn Plaza, New York, NY   10001
(212) 807-8400 • fax: (212) 627-1451
website: www.amnestyusa.org

Founded in 1961, Amnesty International is a grassroots activist organization that aims to free all nonviolent people who have been imprisoned because of their beliefs, ethnic origin, race, or gender. Amnesty International USA makes its reports, press releases, and fact sheets available through its website, including the report "Threat and Humiliation: Racial Profiling, National Security, and Human Rights in the United States."

Cato Institute

1000 Massachusetts Ave. NW, Washington, DC   20001-5403
(202) 842-0200 • fax: (202) 842-3490
website: www.cato.org

Cato Institute is a public policy research foundation dedicated to limiting the role of government, protecting individual liberties, and promoting free markets. The institute commissions a variety of publications, including books, monographs, briefing papers, and other studies. Among its publications are the quarterly magazine *Regulation*, the bimonthly *Cato Policy Report*, and articles such as "School Discipline Biased Toward Minorities."

Center for American Progress

1333 H St. NW, 10th Floor, Washington, DC   20005
(202) 682-1611
website: www.americanprogress.org

The Center for American Progress is an independent nonpartisan educational institute dedicated to improving the lives of Americans through progressive ideas and action. The Center for American Progress aims to develop new policy ideas, critique the policy that stems from conservative values, challenge the media to cover certain issues, and shape the national debate. The center publishes numerous research papers that are available at its website, including "The Voting Rights Playbook."

Council on American-Islamic Relations (CAIR)
453 New Jersey Ave. SE, Washington, DC   20003
(202) 488-8787 • fax: (202) 488-0833
website: www.cair.com

The Council on American-Islamic Relations is a Muslim civil liberties and advocacy group focused on both bridging the gap between Muslim and non-Muslim Americans and protecting the rights of Muslims in the United States. CAIR regularly meets and works with law enforcement and members of the federal, state, and local governments in order to facilitate communication with US Muslim communities to raise awareness of issues affecting Muslims. The CAIR website includes reports, surveys, public service announcements, and press releases on issues of specific concern to American Muslims and on Islam-related topics of general interest.

Human Rights Watch (HRW)
350 Fifth Ave., 34th Floor, New York, NY   10118-3299
(212) 290-4700 • fax: (212) 736-1300
e-mail: hrwnyc@hrw.org
website: www.hrw.org

Human Rights Watch is dedicated to protecting the human rights of people around the world. HRW investigates human rights abuses, educates the public, and works to change policy and practice. Among its numerous publications is the report "Within Reach: A Roadmap for US Immigration Reform that Respects the Rights of All People."

Leadership Conference on Civil and Human Rights
1629 K St. NW, 10th Floor, Washington, DC   20006
(202) 466-3311
website: www.civilrights.org

The Leadership Conference on Civil and Human Rights is a coalition of over two hundred national human rights organizations. The conference works toward the goal of a more open and just society. It publishes the annual *Civil Rights Monitor* and numerous reports, such as "Restoring a National Consensus: The Need to End Racial Profiling," which are available at its website.

National Association for the Advancement of Colored People (NAACP)
4805 Mt. Hope Dr., Baltimore, MD   21215
(877) 622-2798
website: www.naacp.org

Founded one hundred years ago, the National Association for the Advancement of Colored People is the oldest civil rights organization in the United States. Its primary focus is the protection and enhancement of the civil rights of African Americans and other minorities. Working at the national, regional, and local levels, the organization educates the public on the adverse effects of discrimination; advocates legislation; and monitors enforcement of existing civil rights laws. The NAACP publishes *Crisis*, a bimonthly magazine, and provides press releases on its website.

National Urban League (NUL)
120 Wall St., New York, NY   10005
(212) 558-5300 • fax: (212) 344-5332
website: www.nul.org

The National Urban League is a historic civil rights organization dedicated to economic empowerment in order to elevate the standard of living in historically underserved urban communities. The National Urban League has ninety-five affiliates serving three hundred communities, in thirty-five states and the District of Columbia, providing direct services. It publishes the annual "State of Black America" and other reports.

Bibliography

Books

Martha R. Bireda — *Cultures in Conflict: Eliminating Racial Profiling.* Lanham, MD: Rowman & Littlefield, 2010.

Michael L. Birzer — *Racial Profiling: They Stopped Me Because I'm—.* Boca Raton, FL: CRC Press, 2013.

David Boonin — *Should Race Matter?: Unusual Answers to the Usual Questions.* New York: Cambridge University Press, 2011.

Donathon Brown and Amardo Rodriguez — *When Race and Policy Collide: Contemporary Immigration Debates.* Santa Barbara, CA: Praeger, 2014.

Gloria J. Browne-Marshall — *Race, Law, and American Society: 1607–Present.* New York: Routledge, 2013.

Sheryll Cashin — *Place, Not Race: A New Vision of Opportunity in America.* Boston: Beacon Press, 2014.

Joshua Takano Chambers-Letson — *A Race So Different: Performance and Law in Asian America.* New York: New York University Press, 2013.

Joseph Collum — *The Black Dragon: Racial Profiling Exposed.* Sun River, MT: Jigsaw Press, 2010.

Elizabeth Comack — *Racialized Policing: Aboriginal People's Encounters with the Police.* Winnipeg, Canada: Fernwood Publishing, 2012.

Anthony Cortese — *Contentious: Immigration, Affirmative Action, Racial Profiling, and the Death Penalty.* Austin, TX: University of Texas Press, 2013.

Cynthia Lee — *The Fourth Amendment: Searches and Seizures, Its Constitutional History and the Contemporary Debate.* Amherst, NY: Prometheus Books, 2010.

Kenneth W. Mack and Guy-Uriel Charles, eds. — *The New Black: What Has Changed and What Has Not with Race in America.* New York: New Press, 2013.

Kimberly Jade Norwood — *Color Matters: Skin Tone Bias and the Myth of a Post-Racial America.* New York: Routledge, 2014.

Gregory S. Parks and Matthew W. Hughey, eds. — *12 Angry Men: True Stories of Being a Black Man in America Today.* New York: New Press, 2010.

Stephen K. Rice and Michael D. White, eds. — *Race, Ethnicity, and Policing: New and Essential Readings.* New York: New York University Press, 2010.

Stephen J. Schulhofer — *More Essential than Ever: The Fourth Amendment in the Twenty-First Century.* New York: Oxford University Press, 2012.

Jeff Shantz, ed. *Racial Profiling and Borders: International, Interdisciplinary Perspectives.* Lake Mary, FL: Vandeplas, 2010.

Michael Tonry *Punishing Race: A Continuing American Dilemma.* New York: Oxford University Press, 2011.

Tim Wise *Colorblind: The Rise of Post-Racial Politics and the Retreat from Racial Equity.* San Francisco: City Lights Books, 2010.

Periodicals and Internet Sources

Ari Berman "Texas Voter ID Law Discriminates Against Women, Students, and Minorities," *Nation*, October 23, 2013.

Arian Campo-Flores "Arizona's Immigration Law and Racial Profiling," *Newsweek*, April 26, 2010.

Matthew M. Chingos "Are Minority Students Harmed by Affirmative Action?," *Brown Center Chalkboard*, March 7, 2013. www.brookings.edu.

Ta-Nehisi Coates "It's the Racism, Stupid," *Atlantic*, July 23, 2013.

Andrew Cohen "How Voter ID Laws Are Being Used to Disenfranchise Minorities and the Poor," *Atlantic*, March 16, 2012.

Shikha Dalmia	"Asian-Americans in California Send a Message: Race and Gender Preferences Are Obsolete," *Washington Examiner*, March 20, 2014. www.washingtonexaminer.com.
Ben Eidelson	"Liberals Are Making the Wrong Case Against Racial Profiling," *Salon*, May 9, 2010. www.salon.com.
Justin Elliott	"Racial Profiling on an 'Industrial Scale,'" *Salon*, October 22, 2011. www.salon.com.
Renee Feltz	"A Double Standard on Racial Profiling," *American Prospect*, October 5, 2010. www.prospect.org.
Conor Freidersdorf	"Conservative Hypocrisy on Racial Profiling and Affirmative Action," *Atlantic*, July 24, 2013.
Daniel Garza	"Minimum Wage Hikes Hurt Minorities," *Orange County Register*, March 17, 2013.
Alan Gomez	"Racial Profiling Difficult to Prove, Experts Say," *USA Today*, July 11, 2012.
Daniel Greenfield	"Do Background Checks of Gun Owners Discriminate Against Minorities?," *FrontPage*, February 21, 2013. www.frontpagemag.com.
Nat Hentoff	"School Discipline Biased Toward Minorities," Cato Institute, March 13, 2012. www.cato.org.

Kenneth Jost   "Profiling Seen in 'Shopping While Black' Incidents," *CQ Researcher*, November 22, 2013.

Sergey Kadinsky, Tom Namako, and Dan Mangan   "Taxi Big: Fair to Profile," *New York Post*, December 7, 2010.

Aaron Kearney   "Why We Need ERPA: Racial Profiling Lingers Amidst Proof of Targeting," CAIR-Chicago, August 6, 2012. www.cairchicago.org.

Mark A.R. Kleiman   "Smart on Crime," *Democracy: A Journal of Ideas*, no. 28, Spring 2013.

Heather Mac Donald   "How to Return New York City to the Street Gangs," *Wall Street Journal*, August 11, 2012.

Brentin Mock   "DOJ Texas Voter ID Ruling Is No Surprise Given State's Faulty 'Colorblind' Policies," *Colorlines*, March 13, 2012. www.colorlines.com.

Asra Q. Nomani and Hassan Abbas   "Is Racial or Religious Profiling Ever Justified?," *New York Times Upfront*, April 18, 2011. http://teacher.scholastic.com/scholasticnews/indepth/upfront.

Ahmed Rehab   "Why Racial Profiling Makes for Dumb Security," *Huffington Post*, January 7, 2010. www.huffingtonpost.com.

Richard Sander and Stuart Taylor Jr.   "The Painful Truth About Affirmative Action," *Atlantic*, October 2, 2012.

Ilya Shapiro

"*Shelby County* and the Vindication of Martin Luther King's Dream," *New York University Journal of Law & Liberty*, vol. 8, no. 1, 2013.

Keeanga-Yamahtta Taylor

"A Verdict on Racial Profiling? A Judge Has Ruled Stop-and-Frisk Unconstitutional and Racist. But Will It Stop?," *In These Times*, August 16, 2013. www.inthesetimes.com.

Ian Tuttle

"Justice for the System: There Is No Institutional Racism in Our Courts and Police Stations," *National Review*, August 19, 2013.

Dawud Walid

"End Racial Profiling Act: A Smarter Policy," *Huffington Post*, May 3, 2012. www.huffingtonpost.com.

Tova Wang

"Misidentified Priorities," *American Prospect*, January 3, 2011. www.prospect.org.

Walter E. Williams

"A Minority View: Higher Minimum Wage," Townhall, February 27, 2013. www.townhall.com.

Index

A

ABC News, 81
Academically Adrift study, 94
Adkins, Daniel, 20
Affirmative action
　benefits of, 98–99
　compassionate action needed,
　　99–100
　future of, 90–96
　hardship vs. race, 97–100
　minorities and, 97–98
　public opinion on, 81–84
　student help from, 85–89
African Americans
　criminal justice system bias,
　　17–20
　marijuana war and, 23–26
　in prison, 11–14
　slavery of, 7
　unemployment rates, 43
　voter ID laws, 57
Alito, Samuel, 90
American Civil Liberties Union
　(ACLU), 21–28, 76
Arizona Senate Bill 1070. *See* Support Our Law Enforcement and
Safe Neighborhoods Act
Arum, Richard, 94
Association of Community Organizations for Reform Now
(ACORN), 51

B

Barone, Michael, 36–39
Bates, John, 66
Benson, Guy, 51

Blackburn, Marsha, 46
Bloomberg, Michael, 29, 36
Bouie, Jamelle, 81–84
Brennan Center for Justice, 56–57
Brown, Jeffrey, 33
Brown v. Board of Education
　(1954), 91
Bush, George W., 78, 93
Byrne Justice Assistance Grant
　Program, 25

C

California State University, 94
Call-in approach vs. stop-and-
　frisk, 32–34
Carey, Kevin, 90–96
Carson, Ben, 97–100
Carter, Jimmy, 22
CATO Institute, 27
Clear, Todd, 12
Clemmons, Alan, 58, 66
Cohen, Andrew, 62–69
COMPSTAT data, 25
Crack cocaine laws, 22
Criminal justice system as unfair,
　16–20

D

Daley, Richard, 55
Debose, Craig, 67
Department of Motor Vehicles
　(DMV), 56

Don't Shoot: One Man, a Street Fellowship, and the End of Violence in Inner-City America (Kennedy), 32
Duncan, Arne, 93–94

E

The Economist (newspaper), 41
Edroso, Roy, 47
Elizabeth City State University, 96
Entry-level jobs, 42
Epps, Garrett, 8
Eskow, Richard, 44–48

F

Fair Minimum Wage Act, 45
Federal Election Commission, 71
Federal Prosecution of Election Offenses manual, 77
Fifteenth Amendment, 64, 65
Fisher v. University of Texas (2013), 81, 85
Fourteenth Amendment, 65

G

Ghetto-dwellers, 12–14
Ginsburg, Ruth Bader, 65
Goldberg, Jonah, 47
Goulka, Jeremiah, 53–61
Grutter v. Bollinger (2003), 90, 91
Gun buy-back programs, 34

H

Help America Voting Act, 80
Heritage Foundation, 57, 71
Heroin laws, 22
Holder, Eric, 50

I

Immigration and Customs Enforcement (ICE), 7
Internal Revenue Service, 50

J

Jackson, Jesse, 17–18, 20, 37
Jim Crow laws, 83
John Jay College of Criminal Justice, 32
Johnson v. Miller (1995), 76
Journal of Criminal Law and Criminology (magazine), 18

K

Kane, Jacqueline, 67
Kelly, Ray, 31
Kennedy, Anthony M., 88, 92
Kennedy, David, 32
Kennedy, John F., 55
King, Martin Luther, III, 30
King, Martin Luther, Jr., 30, 34, 84

L

Langan, Patrick, 18
Latino Decisions group, 8–9
Latinos, 8–9, 82
Lauritsen, Janet, 19
Leave It to Beaver (TV show), 46
Limbaugh, David, 49–52
Lindsay, John, 38
Loury, Glenn, 10–15

M

Marijuana war
    enforcement of laws, 24–26
    legalization needed, 26–28

overview, 21–22
racial bias in, 21–28
War on Drugs and, 22–23
Marshall, Thurgood, 92
Martin, Trayvon, 16–17, 35
Meares, Tracey, 33
Metcalfe, Darryl, 66
Minimum wage
effects of raising, 47–48
myths, 46–47
opposition to raising, 40–43
overview, 44–45
raising will not hurt, 44–48
worker facts, 45–46
worker fantasy, 46
Minorities and the law
criminal justice system and,
16–20
introduction, 7–9
minority prisoners, 10–15
racism/racial profiling, 8, 51,
57–59
See also Affirmative action;
Stop-and-frisk issues; Voter
ID laws; Voting Rights Act
Minority prisoners, 10–15, 33

N

National Academy of Sciences, 18
National Network for Safe Com-
munities, 34
National Security Agency (NSA),
50
National Survey on Drug Use and
Health, 24
National Voter Registration Act.
See Voting Rights Act
National Women's Law Center, 45
New York Police Department
(NYPD), 30, 36

New York Post (newspaper), 38
New York Times (newspaper), 31
New York University School of
Law, 34, 56–57
Nixon, Richard, 54
No Child Left Behind Act, 93
Northwest Austin Municipal Utility
District Number One v. Holder
(2009), 72

O

Obama, Barack
criminal justice system bias,
20
minimum-wage proposal, 45
Race to the Top school initiative, 93
stop-and-frisk issues, 37
voter fraud checks, 50
O'Brien, Bill, 58
Office of Financial Management
(Washington State), 27
Operation Ceasefire, 33

P

Pendleton, Hadiya, 38, 39
Perazzo, John, 16–20
Poverty concerns, 42
Public Religion Research Institute
(PRRI), 82

R

Race to the Top school initiative,
93
Racism/racial profiling, 8, 51,
57–59
RAND Corporation, 19

Reagan, Ronald, 68
Recidivism, 33
Roberts, John, 63, 68, 90–92
Roksa, Josipa, 94
Romney, Mitt, 46, 58

S

Sampson, Robert, 19
Sander, Richard, 85–89
SAT scores, 86–87, 99
Shapiro, Ilya, 8
Sharpton, Al, 17–18, 20
Shelby County v. Holder (2013),
   63, 67, 69–70, 74–79
      See also Voting Rights Act
Slavery impact, 7
Sowell, Thomas, 40–43
Spakovsky, Hans von, 57, 70–80
Stand Your Ground laws, 29
Stop-and-frisk issues
      call-in approach vs., 32–34
      growth of, 29–31
      minority protection, 36–39
      reforms needed, 34–35
      use of, 31–32
Stringer, Scott, 29–35
Support Our Law Enforcement
   and Safe Neighborhoods Act
   (2010), 7, 8
Sweatt v. Painter (1950), 92

T

Taylor, Stuart, Jr., 85–89
Tenth Amendment, 64
Terry v. Ohio (1968), 31
Texas Southern University, 94
Three Strikes Law, 13

Thurgood Marshall School of Law,
   94
Turzai, Mike, 58

U

Unemployment rates, 43
Uniformed and Overseas Citizens
   Absentee Voting Act, 80
Union Baptist Church, 33
United States Customs and Border
   Protection, 7
University of Michigan, 99
University of the District of Co-
   lumbia, 94
U.S. News & World Report
   (magazine), 30
US Census Bureau, 73
US Commission on Civil Rights,
   86–87
US Election Assistance Commis-
   sion, 50
US Justice Department, 19, 70, 75,
   77
US Supreme Court, 8

V

Vigilantism, 29
Voter ID laws
      adults without ID, 55–57
      barriers to voting, 59–60
      controversy over, 49–50
      fraud concerns, 54–55
      as minority insult, 51–52
      minority voters disadvantage
         from, 53–61
      opposition to, 49–52
      overview, 49, 53–54

racism concerns, 51, 57–59
   solution to, 60–61
Voting Rights Act (VRA)
   concerns over, 75–77
   congressional action, 77–79
   decision over, 64–65
   discrimination concerns,
    72–75
   justification over, 79–80
   need for, 71–72
   overview, 62–64
   US Supreme court revision
    was right, 70–80
   US Supreme court revision
    was wrong, 62–69
   weakening of rights, 68–69
   winners and losers of, 65–68

W

Walker, Scott, 59

Wall Street Journal (newspaper),
  47, 82
War on Drugs, 22–23
Warren, James, 38
Washington Post (newspaper), 81,
  83
Wayne State, 94
Williams, Stephen F., 73–74
World Health Organization, 24

Y

Yale Law School, 33
Yale University, 98
Young, Coleman, 38

Z

Zero-tolerance policing, 25
Zimmerman, George, 17, 29

Per RFP 03764 Follett School Solutions guarantees
hardcover bindings through SY 2024-2025
877.899.8550 or customerservice@follett.com